CONSULTATIVE SALES POWER
Achieving Continuous Success

Karen Mantyla

A FIFTY-MINUTE™ SERIES BOOK

CRISP PUBLICATIONS, INC.
Menlo Park, California

CONSULTATIVE SALES POWER
Achieving Continuous Success

Karen Mantyla

Quiet Power℠ is a registered sales mark of Karen Mantyla.
Diamonds on Velvet® is a registered mark of Karen Mantyla.

CREDITS
Managing Editor: **Kathleen Barcos**
Editor: **Carol Henry**
Typesetting: **ExecuStaff**
Cover Design: **Carol Harris**
Artwork: **Ralph Mapson**

Copyright © 1995 by Crisp Publications, Inc.

Printed in the United States of America by Bawden Printing Company.

English language Crisp books are distributed worldwide. Our major international distributors include:

CANADA: Reid Publishing Ltd., Box 69559—109 Thomas St., Oakville, Ontario, Canada L6J 7R4. TEL: (905) 842-4428, FAX: (905) 842-9327

Raincoast Books Distribution Ltd., 112 East 3rd Avenue, Vancouver, British Columbia, Canada V5T 1C8. TEL: (604) 873-6581, FAX: (604) 874-2711

AUSTRALIA: Career Builders, P.O. Box 1051, Springwood, Brisbane, Queensland, Australia 4127. TEL: 841-1061, FAX: 841-1580

NEW ZEALAND: Career Builders, P.O. Box 571, Manurewa, Auckland, New Zealand. TEL: 266-5276, FAX: 266-4152

JAPAN: Phoenix Associates Co., Mizuho Bldg. 2-12-2, Kami Osaki, Shinagawa-Ku, Tokyo 141, Japan. TEL: 3-443-7231, FAX: 3-443-7640

Selected Crisp titles are also available in other languages. Contact International Rights Manager Suzanne Kelly at (415) 323-6100 for more information.

Library of Congress Catalog Card Number 94-68200
Mantyla, Karen
Consultative Sales Power
ISBN 1-56052-304-2

This book is printed on recyclable paper with soy ink.

PRINTED WITH SOY INK

ABOUT THIS BOOK

Consultative Sales Power is not like most books. It has a unique self-paced format that encourages a reader to become personally involved. Designed to be "read with a pencil," there are exercises, activities, assessments and cases that invite participation.

The objective of this book is to help salespeople achieve continuous success by being "customer-driven" in every step of the sales process. These steps-to-success include preparation, presentation and service actions to get and keep customers.

Consultative Sales Power can be used effectively in a number of ways. Here are some possibilities:

- **Individual Study.** Because the book is self-instructional, all that is needed is a quiet place, some time and a pencil. Completing the activities and exercises will provide valuable feedback, as well as practical ideas for improving your sales and business successes.

- **Workshops and Seminars.** This book is ideal for use during, or as preassigned reading prior to, a workshop or seminar. With the basics in hand, the quality of participation will improve. More time can be spent practicing concept extensions and applications during the program.

- **College Programs.** Thanks to the format, brevity and low cost, this book is ideal for short courses and extension programs.

There are other possibilities that depend on the objectives of the user. One thing is certain: even after it has been read, this book will serve as excellent reference material that can be easily reviewed.

ABOUT THE AUTHOR

Karen Mantyla is President of Quiet Power, Inc., a Washington, D.C.–based consulting company specializing in sales, marketing and professional development programs. A veteran sales and marketing professional, she started as a part-time sales representative and worked her way up to the top of the sales management ladder. She held several managerial positions including District Manager, Regional Director, Field Sales Manager, National Accounts Manager, National Sales Manager and Vice President of Sales for a Fortune 500 corporation.

Ms. Mantyla's biography is currently featured in the 1995-1996 editions of *Who's Who in the World*, *Who's Who in America*, *Who's Who of American Women* and *Who's Who in Finance and Industry*.

TO THE READER

This book is a step-by-step guide to help you exceed your sales goals. Consultative selling is a pathway to success for the two most important people in the sales process: the customer and the salesperson.

Salespeople need to sell and achieve growth in a very competitive, constantly changing business environment. Acquiring and keeping customers is becoming harder, since a lot of products and services look the same to customers. All kinds of offers are being communicated to your customers and prospects. How do they decide what to buy? And from whom? What can you do to turn prospects into your customers and then keep them?

Consultative selling is the answer. This book will explain what it is, why it is vital to achieve on-going sales success and how to apply it in any situation. Consultative selling is a mind-set. It starts with thinking about the customer before, during and after the sale. This is the path of the book, and it is your guide to thinking about your own sales position.

That old cliché, "He's a born salesman," does not apply here. No one arrives with a tag that says,"Look, I'm a consultative seller!" You can *learn* how to develop the mind-set. You can learn how and what to think as you begin each part of the selling process. Thinking about the customer has no geographical or product/ service boundaries. Whether you sell a car in Detroit or insurance in Tokyo, you are dealing with people. How you treat and value them is often the difference between mediocrity and excellence in your sales performance. Caring about customers and how your product or service can support their success is the mission for every consultative seller. It's a high purpose, but also one that can be translated into what to do and how to do it.

Karen Mantyla

P.S. One thought before we start. People often wish you good luck before you begin something new. You won't need luck to be a consultative seller. Practice these steps, and you will create your own luck.

DEDICATION

This book is a gift of experience leading to success. Special thanks to:

My father, Milton Fischer. My lifelong teacher and the best salesman in the world. Who taught me, when I was 14, "Honey, the worst that could happen to you in sales is that someone will say no."

My mother, Sylvia Fischer. Who was always there when I needed a lift from hearing the "no's." My head cheerleader, who taught me to value each day one at a time. And if I wanted to achieve anything, to do whatever it takes to make it happen.

My son, Mike. With me all the way. His strength is inspirational and helped me at every step.

My two mentors at the Membership Division of RIA, Bill Byrnes and the late Joseph Ardleigh.

My special friend and sales trainer, Marti Ksenich, who reviewed an early draft of the manuscript. Her comments and recommendations were very valuable in preparing the final copy.

My friend and colleague Dr. Susan Fenner, who introduced me to Mike Crisp, and in turn, to all of the great people at Crisp Publications.

All the wonderful salespeople that I've been fortunate enough to train. Especially, Debbie Stelmacki, who followed every step you will see in the book with blind faith. As a result, she has been a top producer every year for over 10 years. She is a reflection of the best in consultative selling.

◆

CONTENTS

CONTENTS (continued)

INTRODUCTION

Everyone sells.

Whether it's to your boss, your organization, colleagues, friends, spouse or children—you are trying to "sell" them something. An idea? Why you should be promoted? Reasons for hiring you? Your opinion, or perhaps the error of someone else's?

You may not think of it as "selling." You may think of it as convincing someone of why they should do something that you feel is right for them. And it can be very frustrating when you try so hard, and they don't do what you want them to do! Or the outcome does not produce the end result that you want!

The concepts and content of this book can be used by anyone but are specifically targeted toward those who make their living by selling. And *consultative selling* knocks out the image of the "slick" salesperson. You've probably seen your share of those.

Slick salespeople are out—who wants to do business with them? Not the customers of the nineties. They demand the best, they can afford to choose from a great competitive menu and they expect great service. And that's just for starters.

This can mean agony or opportunity for today's sales professionals. The sales will go to those who best understand and respond to the demands, pressures and profound changes faced by today's customers, and can help them to achieve continuous success. Consultative selling is not a secret formula or technique. It's not a fancy gimmick. It *is* an understanding of why people buy, how to uncover their needs and how to help them succeed with your product or service. This book is not about selling, per se, but rather a guide to *thinking about the customer* throughout the entire sales process.

INTRODUCTION (continued)

The goal of *Consultative Sales Power* is to help you develop beyond the functional responsibilities of a salesperson and to be seen and valued as an on-going resource for your customer. You'll learn how positive positioning skills will help you pave the way for achieving sales excellence. These skills include:

- Having tips in advance on how to succeed before you walk in the door

- Creating your own sales growth plan to help you exceed goals

- Getting appointments with decision makers; having them want to see you

- Doing an in-person needs analysis; having prospects tell you what they want and show you how to sell them your product or service

- Identifying and positioning to each customer's emotional needs

- Giving your presentation with directed effort toward customer comfort

- Handling objections with a proven path toward getting a sale

- Servicing and keeping your customers for life

When you have this solid foundation of positive skills, each person—the salesperson and the customer—will feel good about the entire sales process.

With consultative selling, everyone wins.

P A R T

I

What Is
Consultative Selling?

THE POWER OF CONSULTATIVE SELLING

Your customers don't care how much you know . . . until they know how much you care.

—Gerhard Gshwandtner
Publisher and Founder
Personal Selling Power, Inc.

Power is a source of energy. Your energy, high or low, often depends on how you feel about doing your job, and the results of your efforts. You will see how consultative selling will benefit both you and your customers. The bottom-line results will energize both of you.

You will:

- See what's most important to customers, and why they remain loyal to consultative sellers

- Learn how to develop a rock-solid mind-set that will help ensure your success

- See how customers can make your job easier, by wanting to do business with you

- Identify consultative sales skills and learn how to start using them today

- Be encouraged to value your competition, and identify ways to use competitive information that will guide you toward closing more sales

THE POWER OF CONSULTATIVE SELLING
(continued)

What Is Important to You Today?

Since the two most important people in the selling process are you and the customer, let's start with how this book can help *you*. Whether you are new to the consultative selling process, a veteran sales professional or thinking about going into sales, this book is designed with you in mind. By understanding the consultative process, learning how to do it and making a dedicated commitment to succeed, you *will* succeed.

What parts of the consultative selling process are most important to you right now? Use this checklist to focus on the areas that mean the most to you. In the beginning, review this checklist weekly. After one month, refer to it monthly. Whether you're new or a veteran sales professional your needs and priorities will change, based on your current circumstances.

Today It's Important That I:	Refer to Pages:
☐ Understand how I will benefit as a consultative seller	19–21
☐ Learn how to develop a consultative mind-set	9
☐ Determine what skills can be improved	10, 22–25, 41–43
☐ Know how to apply these skills to my own job	46–49, 54–57
☐ Find ways to help keep my customers	108–116
☐ Develop a plan to exceed my goals	51, 53, 57
☐ Chart my progress	
☐ Select and review one part of the book to support my progress as a consultative seller	

DEFINITION OF CONSULTATIVE SELLING

There are two ways to define consultative selling. One way is to use the exact definitions from the dictionary for the words *consultative* and *selling*. We will look at these in a moment. But that isn't the best place to start.

The power of consultative selling starts with the *customer's* definition. Thinking about the customer at each step of the sales process will enable you to focus your energies on the person who can buy your product or service. Here's where the mind-set begins.

Power Point: *People* buy; organizations don't. *People* sign a contract or place an order; *organizations* don't. Once you start with this thought, you are on your way to becoming a consultative seller.

The following definition is compiled from hundreds of interviews with customers from every size and type of organization. Whether you sell a product or service, this definition is a great place to start, and it can be used by everyone. The customer's perceptions become the real foundation of your relationship.

From the customer's point of view, a consultative salesperson wants to:

1. Take the time to understand what I want and need

2. Take the time to understand what my company wants and needs

3. Show me how a product or service will help me succeed

4. Sell me a product or service and begin a trust-oriented relationship

5. Provide on-going service to help support my continuous success

DEFINITION OF CONSULTATIVE SELLING (continued)

From the dictionary*:

CONSULT: **1.** to deliberate on: discuss **2.** to ask advice of: seek the opinion of: apply to for information or instruction

CONSULTATIVE: **1.** having the privilege or right of conference **2.** advisory

SELL: **1.** to achieve a sale: find a buyer

SELLING: **1.** the act, process or art of offering goods for sale

Based on these definitions, what do you think are the major differences between the customer's perception (definition) and the technical descriptions from the dictionary?

_____

_____

_____

_____

Based on the differences stated above, how do you see them helping you start a positive relationship with a new prospect, or strengthen existing relationships with your current customers? (If, at this point, you can't see how they can help you, don't be concerned. You will uncover the how's throughout this book.)

_____

_____

_____

_____

_____

*Webster's *Third New International Dictionary of the English Language*, unabridged, 1968.

Now, here are the author's comments about the two definitions of consultative selling:

► The important difference is that the customer's definition is based on *their* wants and needs. It describes an emotional picture of what they expect from a salesperson.

► The technical definition describes the process, primarily from *your* vantage point, and does not contain any reference to the emotional side of selling.

► Discovering the emotional needs of your customer, and presenting to those needs, are two very important steps in the consultative selling process.

Consultative Selling Definition Summary:

• Understand what the customer wants and/or needs.

• Understand the goals of the customer and his/her organization.

• Offer product or service recommendations, based on that knowledge (not on what you want to sell).

• Keep in touch with customers to ensure that they are satisfied.

• Care about their current and continuous success.

WHAT IS A MIND-SET?

Now that you know what customers expect, how can you give yourself the best start? Allow yourself to develop a consultative mind-set. Let's take a look at what a mind-set is, and then what you can do to get yourself going in the right direction.

Each individual develops a way of thinking about things that happen in life. Past experiences form the basis of how you think, act or react to a person, activity or situation. New situations or opportunities, like consultative selling, provide a need to develop a whole new way of thinking.

A mind-set is your foundation for actions, reactions and deliberate approaches to any given situation. The organized conscious and unconscious adaptive activities are set by each individual. A negative mind-set often develops when you've had bad experiences. For example, let's say that your product or service can help the financial officer in any organization. You've tried several times but can't make a sale. You may say to yourself, "I'm not going to waste my time calling on them anymore. They never buy."

You've developed the mind-set that they won't buy. And they won't— because you have eliminated them from your list of prospects. If you know that what you sell will help them, but you don't take the time to understand why they don't buy, you both lose. You lose selling opportunities, and those financial officers will buy from someone else, because you have developed a negative mind-set.

On the positive side, you may have had wonderful experiences in selling to plant managers. Your natural inclination, then, is to look forward to calling on them, presenting to them and feeling confident that you have a good chance to get an order. You feel positive about your opportunities. You prepare lists of prospects, you're skilled at getting appointments, and you are enthusiastic during your presentation. You have developed a positive mind-set about selling to plant managers.

Power Point: You have the capacity to set your mind on what you want to do. You determine your own mind-set. You set the rules of thinking, perceiving, feeling and acting in a certain manner.

How Do You Develop a Consultative Mind-Set?

1. Begin by acknowledging that you can learn how to be a consultative seller.

2. Position the fact that you are the person who can best help your customer.

3. Read and memorize the definition of a consultative seller as viewed by the customer.

4. Make a dedicated commitment to learn, and practice the skills needed for consultative success.

5. Set a plan to succeed, and be flexible in your efforts to make it happen.

6. Ask yourself each day, What can I do to a help a customer?

WHAT IS A MIND-SET? (continued)

Exercise: Are You on Target?

Use the terms defined in this section to determine where you are right now. An honest rating of yourself in the following chart will help you begin to focus on your role as a consultative seller.

In Dealing with Customers and Prospects, I:

Point value:	5 Always	4 Often	3 Sometimes	2 Rarely	1 Never
Have a consultative mind-set					
Want to take the time to: • Understand what they want • Understand what they need • Understand the needs and goals of their company					
Value their time					
Discuss what is important to them					
Sell them what *they* want					
Care about how *they* succeed with what I've sold them					
Earn their trust					
Provide on-going service to ensure that all is going well					
Care about their continuous success					

TOTAL POINTS: _____

If you scored above 40, you have an excellent foundation in place to achieve success as a consultative seller. If you rated between 30 and 40, you have a good start and can work toward achieving greater success. A total under 30 indicates one of two things: Either you don't know how to achieve sales success (this book can help you) or you should not be in a sales position.

Many consultative sellers may use this rating as a confirmation that they are on target. And they want to stay there! If your sales results are not exactly where you would like them to be, improvement in one or two areas can make a major difference between average sales performance and exceeding your goals.

New sales professionals may use this as a starting point to understand the most important aspects of consultative selling.

Power Point: Whatever you do, always think about what you are doing *through the eyes of the customer.*

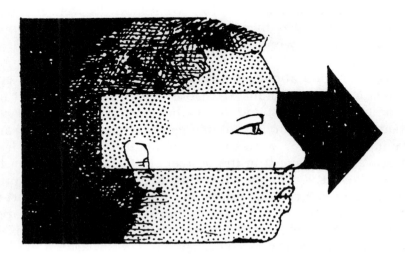

WHAT CONSULTATIVE SELLING MEANS TO CUSTOMERS

This is the mind-set the customer has about *you*. Once you show your customers that you have their best interests in mind, many wonderful things happen.

► **They are more relaxed.** There's almost a sigh of relief. The "sleazy" image of a salesperson disappears. They welcome you without having to hold on to their wallets. The on-guard switch is turned off. They feel good about doing business with you. You are interested in their success and they know it. A consultative seller's customer doesn't think, every time you call, "What is she trying to sell me now?" They know you won't give them a sales pitch because you need one more sale to be #1 or to win a contest, or because selling them something is in *your* best interests, not theirs.

► **They trust you.** Customers will be more receptive to listening to you if you have helped them with a profitable sales recommendation and/ or excellent service. They will be more open-minded, even if they are not quite sure they want what you are offering. Customers of consultative sellers want to hear about what you have, knowing that the "what's in it for me?" is targeted for *them*.

► **They have confidence in you.** You have demonstrated that you know what they want and can give it to them. Your recommendations are based on *their* needs, and what you sell works well. If it doesn't, you quickly correct it with another product or expanded personal service. They know you won't disappear if things go wrong.

► **They feel good about spending dollars with you.** Every customer wants to make profitable decisions. If they have a budget for your products or services, and you've helped them get a good return on their investment (dollar volume gain; increased market share; cost savings, etc.), they want to keep that ball rolling! You're less likely to hear, "I don't have it in the budget" or "I have no money now." They will often let you know when they are in the budgeting process, to get an estimate of your prices and make a conscious effort to ensure that the money is there. And if budgets are cut, which happens in all organizations, they will defend their need and the return on investment they have received from you. They will fight to keep it in the budget.

What Do Your Customers Think of You?

To evaluate your current starting point, write down the names of your three top customers. Identify what you think they value most about you.

My top three customers value me because

1. (*Name of Customer*) _____

_____

_____

2. (*Name of Customer*) _____

_____

_____

3. (*Name of Customer*) _____

_____

_____

Power Point: The mind-set of the customer is that you are a *professional adviser.* You help them make profitable decisions, and they want that to happen again . . . and again.

We can be valued only as we make ourselves valuable.

—Ralph Waldo Emerson

WHAT CONSULTATIVE SELLING MEANS TO CUSTOMERS (continued)

Now, let's take a look at these three customers and identify how they have received a return on investment (whatever may be important to them: profit, increased market share, cost savings, increased productivity, etc.) based on their purchase from you. List as many reasons as you know.

Then, write down what you have done, and *one more idea* you can recommend, in order to build on your existing success.

1. (*Customer Name*) receives a return on investment in the following ways:

_____

_____

Here's what I did to help make it happen: _____

_____

_____

If they did this, it would help them even more: _____

_____

_____

2. (*Customer Name*) receives a return on investment in the following ways:

_____

_____

Here's what I did to help make it happen: _____

_____

_____

If they did this, it would help them even more: _____

_____

_____

3. (*Customer Name*) receives a return on investment in the following ways:

_____

_____

Here's what I did to help make it happen: _____

_____

_____

If they did this, it would help them even more: _____

_____

_____

By "reflecting" on how your best customers value you and what you did to help them, and s-t-r-e-t-c-h-i-n-g to help them with one more idea, you reinforce your value to them. Call or write to them today about that one new idea.

WHAT CONSULTATIVE SELLING MEANS TO CUSTOMERS (continued)

Now let's take a look at several prospective customers who have seen your presentation. They expressed interest but have not given you an order. How do you think they value you? What could you do differently to enhance that value? What new ideas can you take to them that would help them want to buy from you?

Think about it. *They* have thought about it, and they have not bought yet. Were they relaxed? Did they seem to trust you? Did they express confidence in what you were saying—not give a budget objection before you were through with your presentation?

1. (*Prospect Name*) told me that _____

_____

To help them see how they can get a return on investment, I can: _____

_____

2. (*Prospect Name*) told me that _____

_____

To help them see how they can get a return on investment, I can: _____

_____

3. (*Prospect Name*) told me that _____

_____

To help them see how they can get a return on investment, I can: _____

_____

To help ensure that your customers and prospects develop a good mind-set about you, go back to the definitions of consultative selling and mind-set. Use those definitions to strengthen your next sales presentation. It will mean a lot to your customers.

HOW TO EXCEED YOUR SALES GOALS

Consultative selling will change the way you think about selling. And, in turn, you will:

- Retain more customers

- Turn more prospects into customers

- Have customers that are receptive to your calls

- Receive more referrals

- Have customers call you

- Help reduce sales stress

- Make more money

Let's face it: We're in a very competitive sales environment. The pressure is on to get the numbers. Meeting quotas and closing sales are part of the daily mental gymnastics of most salespeople. You are paid to get results.

Many times, these goals stretch the wrong sales muscles. People think too much about selling. What can I sell? To whom can I sell? How much can I sell? How can I get someone to buy from me? How can I get them to buy more?

Many times veterans find themselves focusing on these thoughts, and their sales go down. What is wrong is that they are thinking mainly about themselves, not the customer. Often, what prevents us from exceeding our sales goals is one word in this sentence: *us.*

Consultative selling will help you put goals in a different perspective.

HOW TO EXCEED YOUR SALES GOALS
(continued)

What's Your Perspective Now?

When you hear the word *goal*, the following thoughts may occur. Check the ones that you currently have or have had before.

☐ If I make my quota, I will be very happy.

☐ I'm competitive. I'll beat everyone!

☐ Piece of cake. No problem.

☐ Who set these goals?

☐ I'll never make it.

☐ No one asked me for my opinion.

☐ These goals are impossible.

☐ I can exceed my goals.

Can you identify any customer-oriented thoughts from the above list? That's a major missing ingredient for helping to exceed goals. If you have these thoughts, your next step is to ensure that you shift your focus to your customers. In the beginning, this will be hard to do.

> **Power Point:** Every time you think about yourself, follow that thought with something that you can do to help a current customer or a prospect. This is an exercise for the mind. Your mental gymnastics should always include the needs of your customers.

The expertise of the consultative seller is to always link your goals with those of your customer. Your actions will then lead to discovering customer needs and providing solutions. You will find that providing a product or service to help your customers achieve their goals will always be a step toward achieving yours.

Benefits of Customer-Driven Efforts

When customers feel that they are dealing with a salesperson who cares about their success, many wonderful things happen. Most often

They Look Forward to Speaking to You

Consultative sellers often work by appointment and/or contact their customers on a regular basis. Since phone contact is very important, a frustrating part of the sales process may be when you can't reach your customer. Frequent voice-mail messages (and so many call-back requests that their computer practically recognizes your voice!); "She's in a meeting"; "He just stepped out". . . All this can cause a great deal of anxiety for the salesperson. But the classic situation—when the assistant asks your name, puts you on hold and comes back with "He's unavailable, not in, on vacation, not interested"—usually does not happen to a consultative seller.

They Want to See You

Your customers know that you're there to provide service, and will not hide behind the file cabinets when the receptionist announces your arrival. They are less likely to cancel appointments at the last minute, because their time with you is always productive, in one way or another.

You Will Receive More Referrals

Satisfied customers tell their friends and associates about good service. Getting new customers is not easy, but the good news is that referrals are the best source for making this happen. In addition, your chances of closing a sale with a referral increases dramatically, based on the pre-selling done by your existing customer.

More Referrals = More Receptive Prospects = More Sales

HOW TO EXCEED YOUR SALES GOALS
(continued)

You are Positioned as an Adviser to Your Customer

As such, you will most likely be called when a need or opportunity arises to use your service or product. You will receive more incoming calls requesting information and/or placing orders.

You Will Have Less Sales Stress

When you are a consultative seller, you've still got numbers to meet and fires to put out—but you handle them differently. You feel more in control, because you make choices that will target customer needs and satisfaction. Stress often comes when you feel out of control, or when you can't control a situation. You *can* control your *choice,* however, on the best way to act or react. When the pressure gets intense, you won't go into sales frenzy, thrashing about like a fish that's just been speared! Calling everyone and anyone, and "telling more than selling" is stressful for you, annoying to customers and usually does not result in any significant sales volume. When the goal is to attract and retain customers, your choices will be focused toward that end.

> **Power Point:** Ask yourself: "What can I do that will be to my best advantage?" Then you choose your next steps. *Your* best advantage will be to find ways to help your *customers* and to contact more prospects.

You Will Have More Fun

You will be more confident, enthusiastic, and actually enjoy thinking about solutions to help someone succeed. If a customer has a problem or an opportunity, it's a challenge to think of "what-ifs" that point toward a profitable solution. When you do, it feels great! When you feel good, you keep going, and in the right direction: toward more sales.

So, how else can you benefit besides attracting and retaining more customers? Will you make more money? Count on it. If your compensation program rewards achievement, you'll soon be looking for ways to invest your "unexpected" increase in cash flow. Here's an extreme case: a young woman was hired right out of college. No sales experience. Willing to learn and follow the concepts and content of this book. Her initial sales production was $21,000 per year. In 1993, just six years later, she sold $45 million worth of services.

Power Point: The end result is to meet the goals established by your organization. How you get there and exceed them is often the result of helping customers achieve *their* goals.

We have quietly left behind the "me generation" with its selfish approach to living and have slowly begun to rediscover that serving others is, indeed, an essential part of a successful life. We seem to be returning to what earned us the freedom we enjoy today—to our tradition of finding meaning and adventure in serving others.

—Robert Goizuetta
Chairman and CEO
Coca-Cola Company

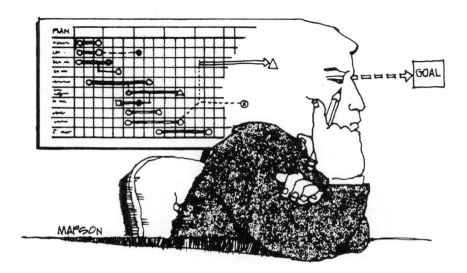

THE DIFFERENCE BETWEEN BASIC AND CONSULTATIVE SALES SKILLS

Two principal skill areas form the solid foundation for your consultative success: basic sales skills and consultative sales skills.

BASIC SALES SKILLS are the tactical skills that are required to do your job. Most sales positions require that you become knowledgeable in these areas. In addition, each organization and/or industry will have very specific learning objectives, to ensure that you learn everything that is of importance to your organization and the markets you serve.

Learning effective ways to implement these basic skills is a prerequisite for consultative selling. In Part Two, you will have the opportunity to begin a self-assessment for the basics. At that time, you can begin to discuss your specific growth needs with your manager. Here is a list of basic sales skills:

JOB KNOWLEDGE

- Company background, history, mission, vision
- Product knowledge; service knowledge
- Sales goals
- Markets for distribution/sales
- Knowledge of the competition

BUSINESS ABILITY

- Time management
- Territory management
- Record keeping
- Profitable selling
- Goal monitoring

SELLING SKILLS

- Prospecting
- Getting appointments
- Probing
- Individual and group presentations
- Handling objections
- Closing
- Call-back presentations
- Getting referrals
- Servicing
- Communication skills (written and verbal)

CONSULTATIVE SALES SKILLS are the skills of an excellent adviser. They include:

✔ *A Customer-Centered Attitude*

Put your customer in the center. Leave your ego at home. Actions and reactions should start with the end goal: the best possible outcome for your customer, and profitable results for your organization.

What do you think about before walking into a sales call?

_____

_____

✔ *Ability to Listen*

Customers should do approximately 80% of the talking. By listening to what they want and what they need, you'll be in a better position to help them succeed. And ask intelligent follow-up questions. The result? You will know how to tailor your presentation to meet the desired outcome for the customer. Next time you make a sales call, think: "If I listen more, I may walk out with not only a sale, but a bigger sale than I expected."

On your current sales calls, who usually does most of the talking? _____

How does this benefit the customer? _____

_____

_____

_____

THE DIFFERENCE BETWEEN BASIC AND CONSULTATIVE SALES SKILLS (continued)

✔ *Flexibility and Adaptability*

You usually know what you want to do before you meet with a customer. Yes, of course, get the sale or get closer to the sale. You've prepared your plan of action. You walk in, and an unexpected problem or situation throws your plan out of whack—now what? Remember to ask yourself that all-important question: "What can I do that will be to my best advantage?" Don't think in ink. Everything can change by the nanosecond. Need to reschedule your appointment because your customer has an emergency? Do it. Don't give your presentation in five minutes. You are worth more than that . . . and so is your customer.

When an unexpected situation disrupts my plan, I _____

How does this help you sell more? _____

✔ *Impatiently Patient*

We are an "I want it NOW" crowd. We want to make it happen. Many times, your schedule for results does not coincide with the realities of what is happening to your customers. Organizations are constantly changing, like a kaleidoscope. Just when you think you are making the last sales call to close that sale—Zap! The decision maker has been fired. Groan. You have to start all over. Or the budget that should have been approved a month ago has another round of cuts before the final word. Or more competitive bids are coming to the customer. You are asked to wait. Do you have a sense of urgency? That's great—keep the fire lit, but don't burn the customer with your blaze! Let the customer know—both the decision maker and his or her staff—that your role is to help provide the best product or service. And that you will stay in touch. You believe what you are offering will serve them well. You will work within their time frame, whenever possible, to help them do business with you.

Just when you think a sale is about to close, it doesn't. What can you do to help your customer? _____

_____

✔ *Solutions-Oriented Thinking*

Help your customers by showing them how your product or service will help them achieve individual as well as organizational goals. A lot of people have ideas, but few people offer solutions. You will position yourself as a valuable adviser if you offer profitable ways to use your product, based on what your customer wants to achieve . . . or needs. And don't leave it to their imagination to figure it out. Let's say you sell a motivational product (posters, plaques, etc.). Your customer wants to reward employees for achievement. Instead of just showing your line and how beautiful it is, take your customer on a mental journey. You might say, "These can also be used in the employee's home. Just think how wonderful it would be, if this were important to the person, to be recognized in front of the family. What great recognition and motivation for continuing to achieve . . ."

Select a prospect who has not bought . . . yet. Based on what you have learned, what kind of solutions-oriented thinking could you try?_____

_____

The skills outlined above take time to learn and practice. Also, let's not forget that we are not perfect. It's unlikely that you will do everything right, all of the time. Don't focus so intently that you forget that.

And it's very important to keep your sense of humor. Humor, though not listed here as a basic or consultative sales skill, can help both you and your customers. (Customers appreciate that; after all, they're human too.)

Power Point: When your customer is the center of your sales universe, your thinking process changes. Consultative skills target the human side of selling. For real people, in real-world situations, your reactions will determine their actions. It's your choice.

HOW TO WIN IN A COMPETITIVE MARKET

The current environment is filled with an overwhelming menu of competing opportunities for the customer. There are so many choices offered by so many different suppliers, it's a wonder that customers get to do any work at all. They are the target for everyone, including you. Offers of "the best in . . ."; faster delivery; less expensive and better quality; great service; and on and on and on.

The global marketplace is only a keystroke away. Being in New York does not pose a barrier to buying goods in Australia. Not only do your customers have more choices than ever before, but the window of competition now circles the globe.

Is this competitive market likely to change? Yes. It will *accelerate*—with new products and services yet to be developed, strategic alliances to help organizations gain new strength, and sharpened skills to ensure that downsizing does not mean losing customers. So, what can you do?

#1: BE INFORMED

Since consultative sellers serve as advisers to their customers, you must establish, monitor and faithfully update your marketing data. Customers will feel more confident about your product and service recommendations if they know you are well versed in who does what, and to whom—for your industry and theirs.

Who Are Your Competitors? What Do They Offer?

Here are some excellent sources of information on the competition:

▶ **YOUR CUSTOMERS.** Consultative sellers always let their customers know that they are constantly researching the market. This is a major credential for offering guidance and advice. Become familiar with what products and services your customers offer, so you can help them serve *their* customers. Work with each one, letting them know that you are always looking for leading-edge information. Ask them, "If you receive anything that might be of interest to you, I would appreciate getting a copy for my file." This helps keep your finger on the pulse of the needs of your customers and their market. And when they send you something, fax a "thank you" the same day.

▶ **TRADE ASSOCIATIONS.** These organizations do research on your products or services and those of your customers. How do you find out about trade associations? Your organization may have all of this information in its marketing department. Use your library, too. A main branch usually has good trade information in the business section. In the United States there are over 20,000 trade associations. You can locate all of them! Ask the business librarian for the trade association information published by Gale Research. Join the trade association that supports your products/services; it's well worth the investment. Read their periodicals, use the member benefits, and if possible, go to their annual conference. In addition to the learning opportunities, you can stop and shop at any exhibitor booth to get the latest information on the competition. If you can't attend, you can usually order audiotapes of the key sessions and ask for any free exhibitor information kits.

▶ **BUSINESS COMMUNICATIONS.** It will serve you well to subscribe to one or two generic business services, to keep up-to-date on what's happening in the business world. Many of these services are available through on-line access or in a print subscription. Some good ones are *Business Week, Fortune* and the *Wall Street Journal.* This will help you to keep on top of developments that might have a short- or long-term impact on your business and your customers.

▶ **LOCAL CHAMBER OF COMMERCE OR CHAPTER OF TRADE ASSOCIATION.** These hometown sources are wonderful. You can attend special meetings based on topics of interest to you. If you travel, there are usually reciprocal agreements allowing you to attend out-of-town meetings, at member prices. You get to network with others to hear what they're doing, what's working and why, what's not working and why not, what the future looks like and so on. Plus, it distinguishes you as someone who is interested in learning about the playing field.

By being informed, you'll gain a competitive advantage by knowing what you're up against; how your product or service compares with the competition; and what specific advantages might appeal to your customers. Consultative sellers devote at least one hour per week to keeping up-to-date.

HOW TO WIN IN A COMPETITIVE MARKET (continued)

After you gather information, prepare the following summary. Be sure to keep it current as new products and/or services enter your marketplace.

My Competitors	What They Offer	Advantages to Customers

(prepare additional pages, as needed)

To ensure that you know every benefit you can offer to your customers, include your own products, services and special handling of customer needs in the summary.

My Product/Service	What I Offer	Advantages to Customers

(prepare additional pages, as needed)

Competition creates excellence. Athletes know the top scores and achievements of the winners. They identify what they can do, and then set out to be the best they can be. Their formula for winning is based on knowing what skill proficiency is needed, knowing the playing field (who's on it and what they can do), and practice, practice, practice.

Knowledge + Skill = Your Winning Formula

#2: KNOW THE FACTS

Customers buy your product or service because they

- NEED it to run their business

- WANT it to help them achieve personal success

- A combination of BOTH

Selling in a competitive environment dictates that you must know customer wants and needs. Be aware of what the competition offers, and be prepared to show how your product will help your customers succeed in *their* competitive arena! You face competition, and so do they! If you do not help them see how their investment with you will fill the needs and wants listed above, then your competitors will. Count on it.

Don't lose selling opportunities because you are too busy to keep informed and sharpen your skills, or because you don't think it's worth the effort. Don't rest too long. You'll be left in the dust as your competitors speed past you on the sales superhighway.

By remembering your role as an adviser, you will win in a competitive environment. You are informed and therefore can make intelligent recommendations to your customer. You are a professional and continually sharpen your skills. You can provide what no one else can offer: a totally professional you, coupled with service that anticipates customer needs.

Power Point: Either you or your competitors will get the sale. Either you or your competitors will retain the loyalty of the customer. The one who offers the most profitable relationship, as defined by the customer, wins.

P A R T

II

Turning Sales Potential into Performance

YOUR FOUNDATION FOR SALES SUCCESS

The people who get on in this world are the people who get up and look for the circumstances they want, and, if they can't find them, make them.

—George Bernard Shaw

We began with the customer and the bottom-line benefits of consultative selling. Now it's time to put the focus on you.

The following is a step-by-step method to help you uncover ways to prepare a sales plan that will help you achieve and exceed your goals. You will:

- Find the common threads of excellence that connect all top producers

- Discover how to connect them to you

- Learn how to capitalize on your strengths

- Use them to help your customers

- Take steps to provide a solid foundation for sales growth

Because everyone is different, we will now look at ways to prepare a sales plan tailored just for you. You will be able to identify what you need to prepare your plan, and tips to make it work.

Finally, you will see how to set up a plan that will benefit both you and your customers.

READ ON TO FIND THE FOUR KEYS TO SUCCESS . . .

FOUR KEYS FOR GUARANTEED SUCCESS

You may be thinking to yourself, "Guaranteed? How can anything in sales be guaranteed?" Is this for real? It is, when you take a look at the profile of a consistently successful salesperson.

Here are the four keys held by every top producer:

1. Positive attitude

2. Extraordinary work ethic

3. Excellent selling skills

4. 360° product/service knowledge

What is so wonderful and real about these keys is that *you* can control your level of achievement for each one! Let's put each key under a spotlight to see where you are right now, where you need to go and how to get there.

1. Positive Attitude

Your attitude can make or break you. As a salesperson, you are more emotionally charged than just about any other professional specialist. When things are going well, you feel great! You don't have to try hard to get yourself "up." You're already there!

Your work puts you in many different situations and causes pressures that are often beyond your control. How can you stay "up" when there are so many things that can bring you "down"? Let's start by examining how you react in the following situations:

SITUATION	HERE'S HOW I REACT
Cancelled appointments	
Can't get in to see enough prospects	
Increased competition	
Pressure from my manager	
Hearing a lot of nos	

SITUATION	HERE'S HOW I REACT

Company makes a mistake with my order _____

Frequent reorganization in my company _____

Frequent reorganization within my customers'
  and prospects' company _____

My product or service is not as good as
  my competitors _____

Add your own: _____

_____

These are real-world, everyday pressures faced by most salespeople. What can you do to help yourself? First, recognize that a negative attitude is often the result of frustration. Having a positive attitude is not easy, especially when appointments are cancelled or a "sure" sale turns into no sale. But that's when a positive mind-set becomes invaluable. You can develop a way of thinking that puts you in control. You can make a list of things you can and can't control. How you choose your next action or reaction to the "can't control" situation will often make a major difference in your sales performance.

Your next move is your choice—positive or negative—and your reaction will determine your action. *You* are in control of the next step.

How would you like to be the next customer contacted by a salesperson with a negative attitude? Think about this for a minute or two. Give yourself a little breathing time to regroup and plan your next step. It's okay to feel down; everyone does at one time or another. It's how you pick yourself up that can make all the difference in the world.

The key question to ask yourself, and one that will sound familiar, is:

What Can I Do That Will Be to My Best Advantage?

FOUR KEYS FOR GUARANTEED SUCCESS (continued)

Successful salespeople are constantly challenged by having to answer this question. It takes a lot of self-discipline and internal motivation to pump yourself up and avoid self-pity. Ask yourself the key question, and think of just *one* way to help yourself with *one* customer or prospect.

For example, let's say you've worked for six months to close a particular sale. It's just about to close . . . you thought. Then you get a phone call informing you that your decision maker has just been fired. Someone else has taken his place. You're told to call back in a month. Here is your action: When a new person is hired, you won't know his or her wants or needs. If you know that your product or service has real benefits for the organization, it's time for you to take action. Send an introductory letter to the new decision maker; include a concept summary of your products or services, a brief highlight of potential benefits and a respectful request to schedule an appointment. Be sure to mention that you will follow up with a telephone call to schedule a convenient time.

You know your own real-life situations. List three negative situations that you've recently encountered. What can you do now that will be to your customer's best advantage? (and yours!)

Here Is What Happened   **How I Can Help the Customer**

1. _____

_____

2. _____

_____

3. _____

_____

Now watch your attitude barometer improve as you start to take positive action that will help you close more sales.

2. Extraordinary Work Ethic

All successful salespeople realize that this is a major key to success, but what exactly does *extraordinary* mean? The key is:

Do Whatever It Takes to Get the Results You Want and/or Need

Extraordinary, as related to sales, doesn't mean that you have to exhaust yourself every day in order to physically show how busy you are. That's not extraordinary, that's kidding yourself. *Doing whatever it takes* means a number of different things:

- Starting earlier in the day

- Devoting time to planning for each call *before* the call

- Scheduling enough quality calls (existing customers and prospects who can buy)

- Following through on service requests from your customers

- Thinking of new ways to help your company market your products or services

- Continuing to give your best efforts throughout the day, especially when you've had success early in the day

- Remembering and following the classic motto, "One more call"

Successful salespeople are not perfect. No one is. If you have a bad day, recognize it as such and deal with it as best you can. Just do your best.

Power Point: The major difference between average and excellent sales performers is that the excellent performers are willing and determined to do whatever it takes to get the job done . . . and done right.

There is no "9 to 5" clock for an extraordinary work ethic. You don't have to be a workaholic or tell everyone how hard you are working. Your work ethic is translated into what you do with your time; how much of it is devoted to achieving customer, personal and organization goals; and your ultimate results. They're all linked together. Just when you think you can't make one more call, make it.

FOUR KEYS FOR GUARANTEED SUCCESS
(continued)

3. Excellent Selling Skills

Earlier, we defined both basic and consultative selling skills. Excellence in both areas will give you an incredible competitive advantage—you'll be the best you can be!

Most times when a salesperson goes into a slump, the problem starts with getting away from the basics. Ask a veteran. An honest answer will usually acknowledge this fact. The key here is:

Having Excellent Basic Skills Is the Prerequisite
for Achieving Consultative Selling Success

You can't have one without the other! Once you determine your proficiencies in each area you can list the skills that need improvement. Discuss them with you manager and your colleagues. Get their recommendations on how to achieve excellence.

Let's look at it this way: When you go to a doctor, there is usually a sense of comfort in knowing this person is qualified to respond to your specific needs. The doctor has graduated from medical school, earned a degree of technical expertise and has on-the-job experience. In addition, every successful doctor keeps abreast of all new medical advances that will help keep patients alive and healthy. Would you want to go to a doctor who was not aware of the latest methods and advances in medicine? Or one who did not take the time to properly identify your specific needs? Would you want to return to that doctor, or recommend that doctor to your friends? Your customers expect your skills to be as sharp and professional as they can be . . . after all, you're their adviser. Don't get rusty!

Excellent selling skills coupled with consultative sales skills equal your "degree" in sales excellence. Like your doctor's, these skills can be learned and reinforced with on-the-job experience. And, like any successful professional, you must always stay informed about any new developments that will affect your sales.

Utilize resources that will enable you to stay informed or learn new skills. Use books, audios, videos, on-line services and distance-learning opportunities (satellite seminars, television, videoconferences, etc.). There is a plentiful menu of learning tools available for use anywhere. You choose! Target at least one resource to keep you up-to-date and refreshed on all aspects of professional selling.

Continually successful salespeople (the key here is "continually") never think they know it all. They know that excellent selling skills are critical to their success. As well, they are eager to learn—from customers, associates, or self-directed initiative—and find ways to stay sharp.

4. 360° Product/Service Knowledge

"360°" means that you know and understand everything about your products and services. Your 360° circle of information includes knowing why your products/services were created (to fill a need?); what they can do for customers; what aspects give you a competitive edge; what customer-support services are in place and how they work to serve the needs of your customers. You come full circle when you learn about what you sell and how it helps your customers.

To top salespeople, "Knowledge is power" is more than just an old saying. You want and need to know everything about your products or services; surface knowledge just won't cut it. Total knowledge gives you the solid foundation to advise your customers on every feature, advantage and benefit of using your company. If *you* don't have all the facts and understand how your products/services will help your customers, how will *they* know?

FOUR KEYS FOR GUARANTEED SUCCESS (continued)

Some important aspects of product/service knowledge are listed below. Check your knowledge and understanding in each area. For any aspect that may be unclear, get the answers from your manager or an appropriate individual in your company. Make this list for each product or service you sell.

Name of Product	I Know It	I Need to Know More
1. I understand why the product was created	☐	☐
2. I know the needs it fills for my customer	☐	☐
3. I know how it is developed and its quality	☐	☐
4. I know the features (facts) about it	☐	☐
5. I can list all of the advantages to customers	☐	☐
6. I know how it compares with competitive products and services	☐	☐

Equipped with this information, sales professionals become credible, respected advisers to their customers. Because you are knowledgeable, you come across as knowledgeable. You can give recommendations based on facts, not hype. Decisions are made on the facts that you provide. If you need to learn more, just do it.

EVALUATE YOUR STRENGTHS

Many salespeople get discouraged about their ability to plan for growth. Their plans usually begin with a "weak" area that needs improvement. This often places them in a less-than-confident starting position. My philosophy is to initiate growth with a strong foundation: your existing strengths. This starts you off with confidence, knowing that you do certain things very well.

Exercise: Chart Your Strengths

In this exercise you will do a self-assessment and identify your top strengths. For each item in the following chart, put a ✓ under the rating that you think reflects your current proficiency. Put a * next to those areas where you are strong NOW!

Ingredients for Success = Current Strengths + Additional Knowledge/Skills

Ingredients	Good	Poor	Strong Now
POSITIVE ATTITUDE	☐	☐	☐
WORK ETHIC	☐	☐	☐
JOB KNOWLEDGE	☐	☐	☐
Knowledge of my company	☐	☐	☐
Product & service knowledge	☐	☐	☐
Markets for distribution/sales	☐	☐	☐
Knowledge of competition	☐	☐	☐
BUSINESS ABILITY	☐	☐	☐
Time management	☐	☐	☐
Territory management	☐	☐	☐
Profitable selling	☐	☐	☐
Goal monitoring	☐	☐	☐

EVALUATE YOUR STRENGTHS (continued)

Ingredients	Good	Poor	Strong Now
BASIC SELLING SKILLS			
Prospecting	☐	☐	☐
Presenting to enough prospects	☐	☐	☐
Probing	☐	☐	☐
Individual presentations	☐	☐	☐
Group presentations	☐	☐	☐
Handling objections	☐	☐	☐
Closing the sale	☐	☐	☐
Call-back presentations	☐	☐	☐
Getting referrals	☐	☐	☐
Servicing customers	☐	☐	☐
Communication skills			
Written	☐	☐	☐
Verbal	☐	☐	☐
CONSULTATIVE SELLING SKILLS			
Customer-centered attitude	☐	☐	☐
Listening	☐	☐	☐
Flexibility	☐	☐	☐
Impatiently patient	☐	☐	☐
Solutions-oriented thinking	☐	☐	☐

Now that you have assembled an assessment of your current strengths, list all the skills you rated excellent and/or those with a star:

_____

_____

_____

_____

_____

_____

You are now going to take this information and translate it into a strategy for immediately capitalizing on your existing strengths, and start creating your own plan for growth.

DEVELOP YOUR GROWTH STRATEGY

Before you begin this section, I recommend that you discuss the previous self-assessment with your manager. He or she wants you to succeed as much as you do—after all, your success is the company's success, too! Targeting your growth strategy, goal setting and planning should all be coordinated with the goals and methods established by your organization.

A strategy consists of preparing a plan toward a goal. Begin by identifying your goals. You need to clearly define what they are, write them down and review them on a regular (weekly) basis. And *take action* to help you reach them.

Your Beginning Strategy Starts with a Realistic Plan

Personal professional development plans often fail for two reasons:

1. You adopt a "one size fits all" model for learning, coupled with recommended, specific time frames for accomplishment.

To help *your* plan succeed, *you* will help design it, based on what *you* want to improve.

2. You try to develop too many ideas at the same time.

People often get discouraged because they don't know where to start. It's kind of like going to a seminar on "51 Ways to Increase Your Sales," or attending a meeting that gives you a wonderful but mind-boggling array of opportunities. What often happens is that you get all pumped up and motivated beyond belief with all of these fabulous ideas or tips. Unfortunately, because there are so many of them, it's hard to decide what to do first. The ideas wind up on a shelf or in a "someday" drawer. Or, you may try to implement a lot of ideas and suggestions, all at once. It's like putting a whole cake in your mouth and trying to eat it. Ugh—not a pretty picture. So . . .

LET'S START WITH ONE BITE!

To help yourself grow, select one or two development areas that are most important to you right now. In this plan, you will give yourself the opportunity to become proficient in just these chosen one or two.

Remember this about your plan:

- You are unique. The beginning of your professional growth plan depends on where you are today. And that's the best place to start.

- Take bite-size pieces in your professional development growth strategy.

Keep these ideas in mind, and your plan (strategy) will be unique, based on *your* starting point, and will be do-able because you will target one or two areas at a time. The end result (goal) is to strengthen existing skills, learn new ones and become proficient in using them. That takes target practice and reinforcement. That, you can swallow.

Your Growth Strategy Starts Here:

Capitalize on Your Strengths

 Improve Your Proficiency in Basic and Consultative Selling Skills

Reinforce Your Positive Attitude

Enhance Your Work Ethic

LET'S START WITH ONE BITE! (continued)

(Capitalize on Your Strengths)

Write down two of your excellent-rated strengths and/or knowledge areas:

_____

_____

and then ask yourself these questions:

1. How have you used these skills to help close a sale? _____

    _____

2. Have these skills helped you secure a new customer? If so, how?_____

    _____

3. What about *keeping* a customer? When did these skills/knowledge
    work to your advantage? _____

    _____

4. Why do you think these skills work so well? _____

    _____

5. What can you do to use these skills with the appointments, presenta-
    tions and/or service calls you make this week? How can they be used
    for the customers' advantage, and yours? _____

    _____

    _____

    _____

    _____

Improve Your Proficiency in Basic and Consultative Selling Skills

It is important that your strategy include several areas that are "open for growth."

List the two *basic selling skill* areas (refer to page 22) that you would like to start with (this week):

1. _____ 2. _____

Which of these resources can you utilize to help you improve your proficiency?

   a. Your manager

   b. Other salespeople

   c. Self-study materials (books, audio-tapes, videos, etc.)

   d. Seminars

   e. Other _____

Write your selected resources here: _____

By when will you do this? (date) _____

List the one *consultative selling skill* (refer to page 23–25) that you want to start with: _____

_____

Focus on developing this skill in every sales call. Think about it before you arrive for the call or before you pick up the telephone. Practice doing this all week. Discuss the outcome of your efforts with your manager or peers: what worked and why, and what didn't and why not. Don't get paralysis by analysis. Think of solutions for improvement and reinforcement.

LET'S START WITH ONE BITE! (continued)

Reinforce Your Positive Attitude

Every day, you have ups and perhaps downs. Answer these questions:

What do you currently do to have a positive attitude? _____
_____

Does it come easy? _____

How do you reinforce it? _____
_____

When it does not work or you are feeling down, how do you pull yourself
up? _____
_____

If that does not work, what else can you do? _____
_____

What one thing do you think would help reinforce a positive attitude? (List
something you can control and/or a choice you can make.) _____
_____

Do it. Keep doing it. Do it even when you don't feel like doing it.

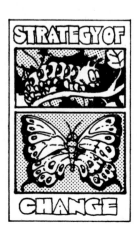

Enhance Your Work Ethic

You can enhance your work ethic by increasing or changing your motivation. Self-motivation is the end result of many different ingredients. Let's take a look at some facts about motivation.

► You determine your level of motivation.

► What motivates you (or not) are these realities: your work environment; your personal environment; your desire to succeed (career and/or financial reward and recognition); what you like or don't like to do; your belief in the rewards of your efforts.

1. Add your own motivators: _____

_____

2. What do you like about your work? _____

_____

3. How does this spark a fire within you to do more? _____

_____

4. Could you do more of it? _____ If yes, what could you do?_____

_____

5. How would this help you? _____

_____

Probably no one loves every aspect of his or her job. Many times, we are not motivated because we dislike certain parts of the job—for instance, setting up appointments by telephone; prospecting; cold calls; administrative responsibilities; objection handling; uncertainty; change; handling complaints. The list can go on and on.

What else would you add? _____

_____

LET'S START WITH ONE BITE! (continued)

Identify Your Demotivators

It's important to recognize any or all of your demotivators and what makes them work for or against you. By looking at them under the microscope, being honest and identifying what you don't like, you take another step toward improving your work ethic! Identifying the problems helps solve them. And it becomes part of your plan for growth and improvement!

My Demotivators:

1. What do you dislike, or what makes you feel less confident?_____

_____

2. What do you do when you face this situation? _____

_____

3. What can help you improve in this area? (something that is within your control or choice of action) _____

_____

4. What assistance would be helpful? _____

_____

Use your ideas for improvement and assistance every day this week. Try them out now; don't wait. Give your ideas a chance to work. Get support from your manager. Use your resources—both people and learning tools—for help. You can do it if you want to.

> *Our chief want in life is somebody who will make us do what we can.*
>
> —Ralph Waldo Emerson

TARGET YOUR SALES GOALS

You've taken the time to identify and focus on what you can do to achieve professional excellence and growth. Now, let's look at your bottom-line responsibilities. What is expected of you?

Salespeople are assigned targets to achieve, and often have additional, higher personal goals as well. High goals are good, as long as they are realistic. Realism means having a solid action plan on how you're going to achieve your target.

Write down your specific goals as determined by your organization, and the time frame for achievement. Write these in ink. If you have additional, personal goals, write these down, too, in pencil. Fill in any areas of the following chart that apply to you, and add any that are unique to your specific job:

SALES GOALS	TARGET	EXTRA GOAL	TO BE ACCOMPLISHED BY (DATE)
Total sales volume			
Number of new customers			
Keep existing customers			
Specific product or service sales (list)			
Increased market share			
Growth of targeted markets			

Additional specific goals: _____

_____

_____

TARGET YOUR SALES GOALS (continued)

Power Points: Keep your goals in front of you. Have them visible everywhere—at the office, at home, on your bulletin board, in your wallet and in your appointment book. You want to see your goals every day.

That way, you develop the mind-set that you can achieve them. You know that you can do whatever it takes to make it happen. You plan to make it happen.

Power Point: Every time you help a customer achieve a goal, and make a sale, you're closer to your target.

Now it's time to put all of these building blocks together into one strategic plan. This will allow you to reach your targets, and give you a very clear crystal ball on how to achieve them.

PREPARE YOUR CONSULTATIVE SALES PLAN

Having a consultative sales plan means taking whatever actions are necessary to strengthen your abilities, to best serve the needs of your customers. In turn, you will achieve your goals. This approach looks at planning from an entirely different angle.

In this section, you become your own adviser. You have identified your strengths, areas for development and personal sales goals. These building blocks are your steps to success. Your climb to the top will be easier once you set up a plan, and take it one step at a time.

Power Point: Your customers should always be the driving force for your plan. You can't make sales without them.

Identify Important Planning Elements

What exactly is planning? It is the visualization of a goal, a chosen course of action to be followed in order to achieve the desired goal.

What's the purpose of planning? It is to identify both opportunities and problems within a time frame, and allow for development and implementation of action steps.

What's the best way to begin? The best plans are simple, easy to implement and carefully prepared.

Now, let's set up the model so you can design your own plan. Here are the four basic steps in planning:

1. Establish the goals

2. Define the present situation

3. Determine assistance needed and barriers to success

4. Develop a set of action steps and a time frame for achievement

The combination of these four steps results in goal achievement. A motivated salesperson without a plan is like a race car driver with a blindfold on. With careful planning, you'll turn your motivation into goal achievement. Planning takes the blindfold off, so you can clearly see your destination.

CONSULTATIVE SALES PLAN

Designed by _____ Date: _____

Note: Use a separate sheet for each of the four plan elements. Set up your plan on a weekly or monthly time frame.

#1: Your Keys to Success

► **Positive Attitude**

How this will help my customers _____

Goal _____

Where I am now _____

Assistance needed _____

Barriers to success _____

Action steps to take _____

_____

I will achieve this by (date): _____

► **Extraordinary Work Ethic**

How this will help my customers _____

Goal _____

Where I am now _____

Assistance needed _____

Barriers to success _____

Action steps to take _____

_____

I will achieve this by (date): _____

► **Excellent Selling Skills**

How this will help my customers _____

Goal _____

Where I am now _____

Assistance needed _____

Barriers to success _____

Action steps to take _____

_____

I will achieve this by (date):_____

► **360° Product/Service Knowledge**

How this will help my customers _____

Goal _____

Where I am now _____

Assistance needed _____

Barriers to success _____

Action steps to take _____

_____

I will achieve this by (date):_____

CONSULTATIVE SALES PLAN (continued)

#2: Basic Selling Skills

How this will help my customers _____

Goal _____

Where I am now _____

Assistance needed _____

Barriers to success _____

Action steps to take _____

_____

I will achieve this by (date):_____

#3: Consultative Sales Skills

How this will help my customers _____

Goal _____

Where I am now _____

Assistance needed _____

Barriers to success _____

Action steps to take _____

_____

I will achieve this by (date):_____

#4: Personal Sales Goals

How this will help my customers _____

Goal _____

Where I am now _____

Assistance needed _____

Barriers to success _____

Action steps to take _____

_____

I will achieve this by (date): _____

Planning for success is an individual responsibility. You are the only person qualified to design your plan. If you want any assistance, there are many ways to get it—people want to help you to succeed, and they are all around you. All you need is the desire to succeed and willingness to do what is necessary to make it happen.

Continuous Business Improvement = Continuous Personal Improvement

> *The greatest thing in the world is not so much where we stand, as in which direction we are moving.*
>
> —Oliver Wendell Holmes

P A R T

III

Preparing for Your Sales Call

PREPARATION: THE KEY TO SALES SUCCESS

You have just completed your plan for specific goal achievement. Now it's time to prepare for the other most important person in the sales process: your customer. Each day, you have a new opportunity to succeed. Preparation will help ensure your success.

This section is devoted to gaining insight and awareness into internal business operations. This is important for both you and your customer. You'll look at various business functions and how your products or services can be used to support different organizational needs. Then you'll explore the emotional buying motives of your customer, to see how and why they influence a buying decision.

Finally, this book helps you prepare for successful consultative calls. You'll identify the most important objectives, for both you and your customer, in scheduling profitable appointments. You will then learn how to prepare sales tools that will help you close more sales.

The Importance of Preparation

> *The best thing about the future is that it only comes one day at a time.*

> —Abraham Lincoln

Even when you have a "bad" day, week or month, you know that new opportunities are available on your next sales call. In order to give yourself the best chance to succeed, it's important to *prepare*. Preparation takes on different proportions based on the needs of your customers and circumstances. Is this a first call? A call-back? Presentation to a group or an individual? Each situation requires its own special plan, which in turn determines your advance time for doing research and preparing for any special needs of your customers.

UNDERSTAND ORGANIZATIONAL NEEDS

Even though "people buy, organizations don't," it's important to be familiar with the basic needs of the organization. When you are, both you and your customers reap these benefits:

- You are knowledgeable about business in general

- You have a basic foundation to think about how your product might benefit their organization

- You have a base of understanding and will know the right questions to ask during your sales call

- You feel more confident when you set your appointments and make your presentations

Here are the basic needs of any organization.

1. *Make a profit.* If what you sell can help make money, save money, increase productivity and/or increase market share, this will be vital to your decision maker.

2. *Successfully manage and integrate key functional areas of the operation.* Success requires knowledge and skill.

MAJOR BUSINESS ORGANIZATION UNITS

There are many functions and specialists within each organization. Our focus here will be on the main functions and departments usually found in every business operation.

- ▶ **Marketing** This function identifies the channels of distribution for the products or services of the organization. Who will buy? Who can buy? Who should buy? Who can help distribute? What methods can be used? Which are most profitable? Where should the geographic boundaries end? Or, start?

- ▶ **Sales** This is the implementation of the marketing plan. Without sales, there is no fuel for growth and profit. In small organizations, sales and marketing are often combined, yet each plays a critical part in any profitable organization. Who will sell? Who can sell? Who should sell? What methods can be used and which ones are most profitable? Salespeople, inside or out, are under intense pressure to produce sales. They are the front line to the bottom line.

- ▶ **Human Resources** The most valuable assets of any organization are its employees. How they are treated and valued can make or break an organization. The Human Resources staff need to know about legal issues; benefits; training requirements/needs; how to foster an environment that values and supports diversity; recruiting, hiring and retaining employees; conflict resolution.

- ▶ **Management Information Systems (MIS)** This unit controls and coordinates the access of information by both employees and customers. With the global marketplace open for business 24 hours a day, technology must provide on-going specific access and support for each functional area in the organization, and ways for each function to integrate its knowledge to support its customers. The MIS staff is responsible for selecting the hardware and software to keep ahead of and anticipate the changing needs of the organization.

MAJOR BUSINESS ORGANIZATION UNITS (continued)

▶ **Manufacturing** For our purposes here, we will define Manufacturing as the group that produces the products or services of the organization. They are responsible for all final aspects of production. They coordinate with other departments to gather new product ideas, and to design, structure and identify parts/services needed to produce the finished product. As well, they must control the quality and quantity needed to satisfy the needs of both internal and external customers. This area usually relies heavily on the use of technology for quality control and increased productivity. If a product breaks or is defective when delivered to the customer, the people in this function often get the blame.

▶ **Finance** This department is responsible for monitoring the pulse of the financial health and profitability of the organization. They get very little recognition, yet they are heroes on the sideline. They must support the entire staff's financial needs by providing information, guidance and direction in areas such as budgeting, compensation and benefits, costs, revenues and profitability. They usually prepare reports to keep each department informed of its financial picture, as well as special reports needed by customers. It is Finance's responsibility to handle all tax requirements and responsibilities with timeliness and accuracy. It is Finance who must often say No to additional budget dollars requests, unless they can see the profitability of saying Yes.

▶ **Customer Service** The Customer Service department is a vital link to customers. This unit is your partner in attracting, retaining and serving the needs of your customers. The staff in Customer Service must handle irate calls and keep everyone calm. Support services enhance the value of the product or service you sell, and can help provide valuable information for securing new business and retaining existing customers.

Your customers have to deal effectively and efficiently within his or her function. He or she must also coordinate with other departments. It's no easy task. This should give you a better understanding of what your customer needs to do, and do well. With this information in hand, you will be able to discuss how, when, where and why your product or service will be of benefit to your customer.

FOCUS ON YOUR DECISION MAKER

At this point, you need to clear your desk and your mind of everything and anything that might distract you. We are now going to look at one of the most critical elements of a buying decision, one you must never forget—not for a minute:

Power Point: People usually buy because of one or more emotional wants and needs. They want their purchase to help satisfy these needs.

You may think that because the customer needs your product or service to run their business, you have a better chance to close the sale. But with all of the competition knocking on their door, why should they want to buy from you? Or, if you have a product that *you* think they must have, but they don't really need it in order to stay in business, how do you help them see why they should buy? In this age of reduced budgets, why should they spend precious dollars on perceived "frills"?

As you begin to focus on your decision maker, understanding the emotional side of selling is vital. You are dealing with people who have emotional needs. Understanding what these emotions are, how to be aware of them and how they can influence your bottom-line results is crucial to having a consultative mind-set. Let's look at some of the emotional reasons people want to buy. As you do, think about yourself and what causes *you* to want something.

Most often, people buy because of one or more of the following emotional reasons. In the following paragraphs are some tips on what these reasons are, how to uncover them and how to manage them as part of the selling process. You will read some visual and verbal clues to watch for in your customers.

EMOTIONAL NEEDS OF CUSTOMERS

1. EGO

Your Clues: You will "hear" your clues. This person will talk about what a great job he or she has done for the organization and/or industry. They stress their value to superiors, subordinates and peers. They talk about their past, present and anticipated worth for the future. They have a lot of pride in their self-worth.

Selling Points: Let them talk about what they have accomplished. Don't interrupt. Compliment them with sincerity on their achievements or value to their organization. Never, never brag about your own achievements or how successful you are. This will deflate their ego and they won't want to listen. Always demonstrate how your product or service will *support* their on-going success.

2. POWER

Your Clues: People desiring power need to be in total control. This person's desk is usually set higher or apart from visitors' chairs. He or she may tell you what to do and how to do it and become frustrated, angry and impatient if things are not done in a certain way. Usually they have major ego needs and they may yell or raise their voice to show you "who's in charge."

Selling Points: Don't be afraid or intimidated. Use your own power to direct your actions. Never invade their space. Do not attempt to go behind their desk. Sit exactly where they request. Position yourself as a professional who "serves the needs of decision makers." Use power phrases such as "This product can be used in the areas that you think need it most" and "You set the ground rules for action. I'm here to be sure that it happens." That way, you reinforce their position of power.

Remember: Never allow yourself to lose confidence because you feel intimidated or less important. They are only human. The worst that can happen to you is that they will say No.

3. PROFIT/GREED

Your Clues: The person will ask questions such as "How will this help me make money?" (or "more money" or "save money"). They will usually ask you this question right up front. Profit/greed is a strong emotional need based on performance for shareholder value, reorganizational pressures, pressures from the top and bottom of the organizational ladder, demands for increased market share—any or all of the above and more.

Selling Points: Immediately demonstrate statistical success by those who use your product. Use phrases such as "increased sales by 30%"; "reduced waste by 43%"; "saved $1 million by . . .". Don't tell these people how happy your customers are or that you are the "leader in your market." They don't care about this, and it will turn them off. Show them bottom-line results. Be ready with testimonial letters that highlight financial benefits.

4. SURVIVAL

Your Clues: These people often talk about the difficult climate within the organization. They often say "money is tight." They are indecisive. Their body language is tense—usually leaning forward and talking at a fast pace—and they appear anxious and fidgety. They are not risk takers and are nervous about making a wrong decision. They are not in an innovative mind-set.

Selling Points: Offer reinforcement that others in their position have valued, used and been helped by your service. Don't tell them your product is new or "leading edge"—that will push you over the edge and out the door. Rather, show them how your product has been successful time and time again. Reassure them that you and your product are proven and reliable.

EMOTIONAL NEEDS OF CUSTOMERS
(continued)

5. NEED TO WIN

Your Clues: This person is competitive and usually aggressive. These high-energy, risk-taking people use the "ready, fire, aim" method of making a decision. Leaders of the pack, they want success badly. They are usually very impatient.

Selling Points: Make sure that what you are selling has some competitive benefit to offer. If allowed by your management, quickly highlight three or four top organizations that use your product. And be sure to point out new or innovative features that will give the customer "leading-edge" opportunities. Your presentation should focus on how this person can get to the finish line faster and, if possible, be a star in their industry.

6. STATUS

Your Clues: Titles are important to these people. They need to know that their superiors value their contributions, and they will work extra hard to move up the corporate ladder. You'll find a lot of workaholics in this area. They thrive on recognition and accolades from subordinates, too.

You can usually sense this need as soon as you walk into their office. Diplomas, awards and recognition letters will be up on the walls, and/or they will tell you about their accomplishments.

Selling Points: Achieving status is not easy in a competitive environment, and they need to be assured that what you sell will, first, help *them,* and *then* help their organization. Tell them stories about people who used your product and how it helped their career shine. Describe how someone used your service; how "their boss was impressed with the results" will fall on receptive ears.

7. SELF-IMPROVEMENT

Your Clues: These people want to do whatever they can to increase their knowledge and effectiveness. You may see lots of seminar completion certificates on their walls, and various self-improvement video courses and books on their shelves. They have a thirst to continually improve and learn.

Selling Points: Find the proper time during your sales call to comment on what you see in their office. They are proud of their initiatives and want you to notice it. Be sincere. Ask them about a particular book or course that you see, and what appealed to them. Ask what subjects they like to explore. Describe how your product or service can add to their foundation of knowledge, help increase their productivity or help others realize their potential.

You can probably put yourself in one or more of the categories listed above. Maybe there are categories that you want to add, based on your knowledge of and sensitivity to your own customers.

Exercise: Identify Customers' Emotional Needs

Write down the names of several of your current customers. See if you can list their emotional needs. This will help foster additional ideas of how you can help them. If you can't identify their emotional needs, wait until your next call. With your new awareness of emotional perspectives, you will be in a better position to evaluate and respond to these needs on your next call.

Customer   **Emotional Need**

_____

_____

_____

_____

The important point is to be aware of the power of these needs in your customers' decisions. If you can spot them, you will gain additional insight in how to best position yourself and the benefits of your product or service.

SET PROFITABLE APPOINTMENTS

As a salesperson, your venture capital is your valuable time, and you want to invest it wisely. This section is devoted to giving you a substantial return on your investment. In order to make sales, you need to see enough qualified prospects and customers, and that means making profitable appointments.

> **Power Point:** A profitable appointment is one that is scheduled with people who can buy or who can strongly influence the sale, or a service call to an existing customer.

So far, we have talked about and developed a plan targeted to help you succeed. Planning for profitable appointments is important, too. If you develop a plan to reach a goal, chances are you will reach it.

Planning to set profitable appointments involves answering three questions:

1. What Is Your Objective?

2. What Are the Methods You Will Use?

3. What Are the Benefits to the Customer?

1. What Is Your Objective?

Check any that apply.

☐ To set an appointment with a prospect

☐ To set a call-back appointment

☐ To set an appointment with an existing customer

Add any additional objectives:

_____

_____

Whatever your objective, you need to write it down. This is your reason for calling. Write one current objective here:

My objective is _____

2. What Are the Methods You Will Use?

Check any of the following that will help you achieve your objective.

☐ Make a list of all prospects who can buy. Add at least 50 new names per week.

☐ Make a list of all current customers and their top three needs.

☐ Prepare a telephone script to use for each specific objective listed above (keep this in clear view whenever you schedule appointments). Many top veteran salespeople carry this with them on the road, so don't think scripts are for sissies—they're for professionals. You won't sound "canned," just prepared. The goal of your script is to get the appointment, not to make a sale. Make your script brief, to the point and full of specific benefits for the customer. Aim for professionalism, enthusiasm and a respectful approach.

☐ Prequalify your prospects and customers. Be sure you are meeting with the right person to help accomplish your objective. (The "right" person is a decision maker who can authorize or strongly influence the sale.)

☐ Block off time during each week that is devoted solely to scheduling appointments. Do *not* give up your "appointment to schedule appointments" except for something truly urgent. If you give up that time, your venture capital starts to disappear.

Add any additional methods you use or want to use:

_____

_____

Now write down the specific methods you will use to achieve the objective identified. The methods I will use are:

_____

_____

SET PROFITABLE APPOINTMENTS
(continued)

3. What Are the Benefits to the Customer?

Why should a customer schedule an appointment?

There must be tangible, profit-oriented reasons for a customer or prospect to give up his or her time to see you. Based on your identified objective, write down the benefits to the customer.

The benefits of scheduling the appointment with me are:

1. _____

2. _____

With careful planning, your time will yield a profit opportunity for both you and your customer. This is why you both should invest your time.

PREPARE CUSTOMER-FRIENDLY SALES TOOLS

It's important to prepare sales tools that will assist you in your sales calls. A tool is a means to an end, and for a consultative seller, that end is a sale to a customer who feels good about buying from you. You want to make your tools "customer-friendly" because they will be used by both you and your customer to reach a successful end result.

The following tools are designed to help you make a focused presentation for selling what the customer wants and needs. With these tools, you will reflect a professional image as an adviser and help focus on top priorities.

> **Power Point:** People make an average of 11 decisions about you during the first 7 seconds of contact!* In a way, *your appearance is the first tool.*

Many sales positions require informality. That's fine—but neat and clean fits anywhere. Carry a professional-looking briefcase, writing portfolio or folder. Don't forget your business cards, pen, back-up pen and your appointment book!

Now let's examine two important sales tools that show the customer that you prepared just for him or her. Treating the customer well from the first, as someone who is important, goes a long way. People don't like to feel they are the recipient of a "one-size-fits-all" pitch.

First Tool: Customer Profile

This will allow you to focus on each customer, and the important things you need to know about them and their organization. A sample Customer Profile form is provided here; you can customize it to fit your needs. Prepare a file folder containing the Customer Profile. Fill out as much of the information as you can, *prior* to your sales call. During the sales call, you will ask for and get additional information. Your goal is to have a completed Profile. Once you do this, you'll have a better understanding of how your product or service can help your customer.

---

*Willingham, Ron. *Hey, I'm the Customer*. Prentice Hall, 1992.

PREPARE CUSTOMER-FRIENDLY SALES TOOLS (continued)

Customer Profile

Organization _____

Address _____

Telephone _____ Fax _____ E-mail _____

Key contacts:

Name _____ Title _____ Phone _____

Name _____ Title _____ Phone _____

Headquarters location _____

Number of locations _____ Number of employees _____

Primary products/services:_____

Major customers:_____

Important business issues (by organization and industry) _____

_____

Mission statement of organization:_____

_____

Specific needs of customer _____

_____

Goals _____

Activity Profile

Date	Action step(s)	Next step(s)	Date needed

This form may be reproduced without further permission from the publisher.

Second Tool: Priority Sheet

This tool will show your customers that you are knowledgeable about their specific function. A sample form is provided here. You many want to ask your manager what to list on your own form, based on the customers who buy your products or services. The Priority Sheet will be used in your sales call to help both you and the customer focus on the most important areas of concern. As a consultative seller, you will frequently use this form to help you sell what your customer wants and needs, so keep a lot of copies on hand.

The author developed the Priority Sheet over 10 years ago. Before its creation, the call-to-sale ratio in her company was 1 out of 16. The salespeople heard a lot of No's and couldn't figure out why. It was because the customers (and salespeople) had not prioritized the customers' issues. It's hard to know what to present when "everything" has top priority, and a confused customer does not buy. After the salespeople started using these sheets, the call-to-sale ratio went to 1 out of 4.

PREPARE CUSTOMER-FRIENDLY SALES TOOLS (continued)

Priority Sheet

The following are the current and anticipated priorities of executives like yourself.

☐ Reducing the costs related to health care

☐ Developing a total quality commitment with all employees

☐ Increasing market share for existing and new products

☐ Maintaining position of excellence in customer service

☐ Encouraging team building in all departments

☐ Attracting and retaining excellent employees

☐ Reducing costs of production

☐ Entering foreign markets

☐ Other _____

Name _____ Title _____

Organization _____ Date _____

PART

IV

Conducting the Sales Call

THE SALES CALL

You're on! You have taken a step-by-step approach to get ready for your customer. You have developed your personal plan and prepared for each individual customer. Now it's time to take your hard work and turn it into sales volume.

We will take a look at each major part of the sales call, from the very beginning, to the time you walk out of your customer's door. We'll examine ways to ensure that the sales call turns out to be of benefit to both you and your customer. Our goal is to use consultative skills at each step, and meet the needs of the customer. Our end result is to make a sale. And we will identify ways to end the call that will help the customer feel good about buying from you.

HOW DOES A CONSULTATIVE SELLER BEGIN?

"Breaking the ice" is often the critical starting point for the success of your meeting. Your goal for the beginning of the call is to have the customer:

- Be comfortable with you

- Want to listen to you

- Value what you have to say

You are the director of your own first impressions. The decisions you want the customer to make, right up front, are that:

- You are a professional—in image, knowledge and communication skills.

- You have the customer's best interests in mind.

- You are enthusiastic and believe in the benefits of what you are selling.

Tips to Help You Begin

► Greet your customer by name—and get it right! Everyone loves to hear their own name, but not when it's mispronounced.

► Show respect for every person you meet. Respect is a universal sign of goodwill.

► Be informed and sensitive to the needs of cultural environments different from yours. If you go outside of your own community or country, take the time to research the customs and ways of doing business there. This is critical and will be an instant reflection of your respect and your knowledge.

► Tell the customer what you would like to accomplish during your time together. Be sure to tie it in with an advantage for them. (Why should they listen to you? What's in it for them if they do?) This will ensure that you are going in the right direction, and will give you the first Yes. If you are going in the wrong direction, your customer will be able to let you know, right up front, so you can change direction quickly.

Case Study: Easy Does It

Consider the saleswoman who was transferred from a New York City division to a branch in Mississippi. In New York's business world, patience is not a virtue, and salespeople often had to specify a bottom-line benefit before their greeting was complete! In Mississippi, patience was instrumental on every call, and this saleswoman learned the hard way. In the beginning, no one trusted her because she spoke quickly and wanted to get going with her presentation as soon as possible. Her sales were almost nonexistent. She learned to slow down and adapt to the right pace—*their* pace—and her sales improved.

HOW DOES A CONSULTATIVE SELLER BEGIN? (continued)

The following sample script is a universal starting point for consultative sellers. You can take this sample opening and tailor it to fit your needs.

> *"Mr./Ms. Prospect/Customer, I appreciate the opportunity to meet with you today. As I indicated on the phone, ABC Company has a product/service that I believe will be of benefit to you and your company. In order to maximize our time together, I would like to explain the mission of my company, and how we serve our customers. Then I would like to understand what is important to you, your priorities for (type of product/service), and how our product might be of benefit to you. Would this be okay?"*

If they should ever say No, simply ask them how they would like to proceed.

Write down a beginning in your own words:

_____

_____

_____

_____

_____

_____

_____

_____

A lot of salespeople start with small talk before they begin their presentations. Do you talk about the stuffed fish on the wall? The pictures on the desk? The office decor? Okay—but use common sense. Some small talk sounds phony, and customers hear it all the time. Combine common sense with an enthusiastic, benefit-oriented beginning, and you're on your way to a sale.

DO A GREAT NEEDS ANALYSIS

In order to make a sale, you must know what your customers need. This may sound simple, but it can often be difficult to pinpoint what your customers want. Sometimes customers know the exact specifications of what they need and will tell you. Other times they know exactly what they want to achieve but are not quite sure how to get there. And then, at other times they are not sure they need anything at all! It can be frustrating for the salesperson *and* the customer.

Enter the consultative seller: you. Your objective is:

Discovering What Your Customer Wants and Needs

Here's What You Will Need:

- Enough Time
- Customer-Friendly Sales Tools
- A Method to Discover Wants and Needs
- Your Consultative Skills (Review Part One)

A needs analysis includes everything listed above.

Enough Time

Don't rush this part of your presentation. If your customer has an emergency or needs to cut the meeting short at this point, reschedule right then and there. Your words will indicate to the customer the importance of this time. For example, you can say *"Mr. Customer, I'm sorry that we have to cut it short. I understand. I'd like to reschedule our time together to be sure that we discuss your specific needs. Then I will be able to give you all the specific information that targets what you want. How is (day) at (time), or would (day) at (time) be better?"*

> **Power Point:** Do Not Rush! Many salespeople have a tendency to rush if they are being rushed. If you do this, most likely you won't make the sale.

It might take forever to get back in touch, and your customer may make a decision based on the little amount of information that you've already provided.

DO A GREAT NEEDS ANALYSIS (continued)

Customer-Friendly Sales Tools

Have your Customer Profile, Priority Sheet and writing tools in your briefcase. Don't take your writing tablet out yet. That will come soon.

A Method to Discover Wants and Needs

The best method to discover wants and needs is to use your Priority Sheet. Remember: Don't come across like a private investigator. Explain what you are doing and why, and the benefits to the customer. If they're not comfortable, they will clam up.

Let your customer know that you prepared just for him or her. At the beginning of the needs analysis, take out the Customer Profile so the customer will know that you gathered preliminary information about the organization. Your goal is to obtain all the information about the organization that will help you to focus on specific needs. Share your initial data, and ask the customer to help you expand it, as well as to explain the goals of the organization.

After you have gathered information about the organization, take out your Priority Sheet. Here's a simple opening that you can use:

> *"Ms. Customer, in my visits with many (financial officers, production managers, etc.) they have shared their current and anticipated priorities. In order to maximize our time together, I would like to focus on what is most important to you at (name of organization). Is that okay with you?" (NOW, take out Priority Sheet.) "I would appreciate it if you would check off all areas on this Priority Sheet that are important to you. And under Other, list anything that is of unique importance to you here at (name of organization)."*

Note: If for some reason you don't use a Priority Sheet, you must ensure that the customer does most of the talking and tells you what he or she wants and needs. You want to uncover the customer's top priorities. Once you know them, you will be able to deliver a customer-driven presentation.

Sometimes a customer will say, "They're all important." You respond, "I'm sure they are. Which ones take up most of your time?" (focus) Then offer your pen. Be quiet and let them fill it out. This is the first tangible way to identify wants and needs. When the customer is done, review it, and then move to identify top priorities. "Mr./Ms. Customer, of those you checked off, please circle the top three that are most important to you *right now*." (urgency)

Next, you can begin to ask at least two open-ended questions:

- "Of all these areas, why is (state #1 area) most important *right now?*

Based on the answer, ask another open-ended question, such as

- "What would help you make it happen?"

- "When do you think this could be accomplished?"

- "To achieve this goal, what do you feel would make the biggest impact right now?"

Finally, before you end your needs analysis, uncover a long-term (one year or more) question. Here's where you can identify the vision and dreams of your customers.

> *"(Name of customer), let's say it's one year from now. You're sitting back in your chair and you say, I did it—I accomplished it. What did you do?"*

Be totally quiet and listen. Write down the key wants. You have just completed a needs analysis for short- and long-term want and needs.

Remember: Write down all answers on your tablet. Keep the Priority Sheet on the desk between you and your customer; never put it away until you are ready to leave. You will refer to it during your sales call. And keep it in the customer's file for future reference.

DO A GREAT NEEDS ANALYSIS (continued)

When asking questions, listen and don't interrupt. If you interrupt, it tells the prospect that what you have to say is more important. Instead of interrupting, cough! When you ask follow-up questions, don't give off-hand responses such as "That's great" or "Uh-huh" and then quickly move on. It's another red flag to your customer that what they have just said is not important.

Benefits of Using Priority Sheets

✔ Customer begins to participate (positive start)

✔ Helps to focus priorities (wants and needs)

✔ Lets your decision maker know that others face same priority areas (comfort)

✔ Allows you to pinpoint what is most important today (urgency)

The above process has been tried, tested and used by hundreds of consultative sales professionals making over $100,000 per year. This may be a new process or variation on what you are currently doing. Your goal is to make it work for you.

How do you see this working in your current position? _____

_____

How would you adapt it to make it comfortable for you? _____

_____

_____

What one skill would improve your needs-analysis abilities? (There may be more, but just start with one.)

I could _____

_____

Do it. Practice it on all your calls for at least two weeks.

CONFIRM WHAT YOUR CUSTOMER WANTS AND NEEDS

You've just completed your needs analysis and are feeling confident. You have done a great job asking questions, and you've listened to the answers. You wrote everything down. Now it's time for an important safeguard: making sure that both you and your customer are on the same wavelength. This is where the foundation of your presentation begins. You can't proceed effectively without first confirming that you are heading in the right direction.

Let's start by focusing your mind on what to do next. Do any of these thoughts enter your mind before your presentation?

	Yes	No
I hope I can get done by (time)!	☐	☐
I'll show her the "hot" new products.	☐	☐
I need more sales to meet my quota!	☐	☐
I've got to sell something!	☐	☐

Other: _____

Other: _____

At this point, salespeople are sometimes thinking more about themselves and *really* miss the target. When this happens, it is very important that you work toward getting back to the needs of the customer as you are about to begin the presentation, because this gets you back on the *Yes* path to a sale. If you're on the wrong track at this point, your customer will quickly let you know—but you've got to ask.

Power Point: Getting positive confirmation from your customer at every step of the sales process is very important to both of you. You can't effectively proceed without confirming that you are going in the right direction.

CONFIRM WHAT YOUR CUSTOMER WANTS AND NEEDS (continued)

You got your first *Yes* when you asked permission to proceed with the needs analysis. To *confirm* the information gathered during your needs analysis, here's a sample inquiry. Like any example, you'll want to customize it with words that are comfortable for you.

> *"Mr./Ms. Customer, before I review the products/services that my company offers, I want to be sure that I understand exactly what is important to you. Based on that understanding, I will provide you with specific information and ideas on how our products can work for you. Would that be all right?"*

Your second *Yes* should come now. Customers usually do not object to hearing you repeat their wants and needs. In fact, it helps solidify their sense of importance. And, if what you say is not on target, they will correct you. That's fine, too, because it gives you another opportunity to ask more open-ended questions. Continue:

> *"Mr./Ms. Customer, you indicated that your top priorities right now are to (refer to Priority Sheet or repeat conversational dialog). You would like to reduce costs in these areas and help your staff increase productivity with the use of new technology. You need to save money and want to provide new training for your employees. Is that correct?"*

If you get your next *Yes* now, that's a green light to proceed. If your customer says *No*, then you can clarify your misunderstanding. Never say, "But you said . . ." You've got a red light and you need to change it to green. Respectfully say, "It would be very helpful if you would clarify what areas are most important right now." Go back to listening, and then repeat your understanding. You must get confirmation before the next stage of your presentation.

Practice this confirmation process on each sales call. Put a red ✔ on the top of your Priority Sheet or writing tablet to remind you to confirm.

On your next sales call, be sure to confirm, and then complete these statements:

Write down what you said: _____

_____

How did the customer respond? _____

_____

How did you feel when asking for confirmation? _____

_____

What, if anything, would you do differently next time? _____

_____

Do it. Keep doing it. It will make the next step of the sales process so much easier.

GIVE A WIN-WIN PRESENTATION

A win-win presentation means that you help your customer and you close a sale—and that you are both comfortable with the process. This section will give you a solid foundation for making this happen.

Your sales presentation usually has three objectives. To:

- Create the awareness of a problem and/or need

- Demonstrate and confirm that you can help the customer

- Make the sale

Let's take a look at each objective and what you can do to accomplish your win-win sales call.

Create the Awareness of a Problem and/or Need

Here's where you repeat the information received during your needs analysis. Point to the Priority Sheet or refer to your notes, and say something like this:

> *Ms. Customer, you just indicated that (repeat the priorities) are very important in meeting your objectives. I would like to focus on showing you how our (name of your product/service) will help make that happen."*

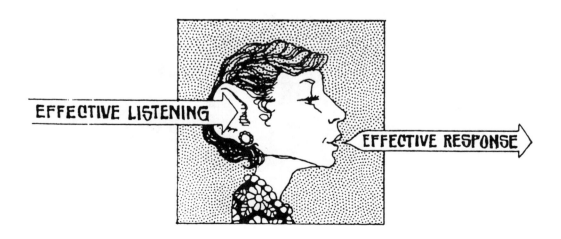

EFFECTIVE LISTENING

EFFECTIVE RESPONSE

Demonstrate and Confirm That You Can Help the Customer

Your customer needs to hear that you can provide a solution to effectively deal with the problems, needs and opportunities that have been communicated to you. It's time to *merchandise* your products and/or services. Merchandising is using a specific idea or information to *illustrate a concept.* Good merchandising creates an environment where the customer wants your product, as well as shows them why they need it. Here is the path you want to follow to merchandise each product, service or program that specifically responds to a want or need. You need to effectively *demonstrate and isolate each product* to spotlight its clear value to the customer.

1. *Paint a picture with words* before actually showing your product. (Describe its purpose.)

2. *Explain* how your products or services fill a need. (Use the needs analysis.)

3. *Describe* the product, how it works and the benefits to the customer. This shows the customer the solution provided by the product—the payoff. (And answer the question "What's in it for me?")

Power Point: You need to effectively isolate and demonstrate each product to show off its clear value to the customer. Don't show everything you've got all at once. The customer may feel overwhelmed or become confused. A confused mind doesn't buy.

GIVE A WIN-WIN PRESENTATION
(continued)

Diamonds on Velvet®

Here's an analogy about merchandising that will illustrate why you must merchandise each product or service, one at a time. It's called *Diamonds on Velvet*.®

Take a dark cloth (I wouldn't expect everyone to have a piece of velvet!), and take a bunch of silver paper clips (who has diamonds lying around?). Dump the clips on the cloth. Pretend these are your products. You are showing them to your customer, and you want them to see everything. It's a bit overwhelming, right? And hard to distinguish one clip from the other. When you dump everything on the customer, they usually want to "think it over."

Now, take away all of the paper clips but one. Pretend it's one product. You show your customer what it is, what it can do and its advantages. It's easier to illustrate all of the features, advantages and benefits of one product—easier for the customer to "see" the one product. It stands out, benefits and all, by itself. You make it special for the customer. It's easier to create the environment for a Yes, because the one item isn't competing with everything else.

Now, let's look at an example of merchandising a product: a special report on marketing. The customer expressed a need to strengthen the company's marketing initiatives, and you have several products that address this. You start with the one you feel is best.

PURPOSE: "Because the business environment is rapidly changing, the need to prepare or update a clear-cut marketing plan is a must."

APPROACH: "This special marketing report is designed to do two things:

1. Provide a step-by-step formula for your marketing plan

2. Provide up-to-date worldwide statistics in all industrial and commercial markets"

BENEFIT/SOLUTION: "This report is laced with specific actions you can take to quickly capitalize on existing and new market opportunities."

CONFIRMATION: "How do you see this working for you?"

Remember to ask for and get confirmation at every major step in your presentation. Every time you merchandise a product/service, you want to see how your customer feels about what he or she has just seen. This will help both of you stay on a positive track. If your customer does not see benefits and give you confirmation as you go along, you'll probably get a boatload full of objections at the end of your presentation. If you are off track, you need to know why. Ask! Then you can quickly respond with better-focused, benefit-related merchandising.

> **Power Point:** Remember to isolate each product during your presentation, link it to its benefits and get confirmation as you go along.

Make the Sale

If you have taken one product or service at a time and received confirmation at each step, you should be close to a sale. It's time to close.

> *"Mr./Ms. Customer, you've seen how (product) can (state need) and help achieve your objectives. I can start this for you on (date). All I need is your okay to get it going."*

GIVE A WIN-WIN PRESENTATION (continued)

It's Your Turn

Think about the calls you made this week. Take two of those, and write down what the customers specifically wanted to achieve. Write down two examples of merchandising your product or service, following these steps:

1. Create an awareness of need.

2. Show how you can fill that need.

3. Tie it down with a benefit (course of action and emotional payoff).

Name of Product/Service _____

Customer Need _____

Purpose _____

Approach _____

Benefit/Solution _____

Name of Product/Service _____

Customer Need _____

Purpose _____

Approach _____

Benefit/Solution _____

TURN OBJECTIONS INTO SALES

Objections can be one of the most frustrating parts of the sales process. Or, you can turn it into a way of identifying *why* your customer is not buying. In this section you will learn an objection-handling process for managing any and all objections. This is not "35 Objections and How to Overcome Them." What will you do when number 36 comes along? You need a way to handle any objection aimed in your direction. Once you've mastered this process, you will close more sales.

Commonly Heard Objections

Check any that have blocked your sales:

☐ There's no money left in the budget

☐ It costs too much

☐ I want to think it over

☐ I want to discuss it with . . .

☐ We already have a similar program

☐ Maybe in a few months, or next year

☐ I really don't need it

☐ I'm too busy now to decide

☐ We're different

Add other objections that you have heard:

☐ _____

☐ _____

☐ _____

There are two reasons why customers usually object:

▶ They are not convinced that they will personally benefit.

▶ They don't see how their organization will get a return on their investment.

Let's clarify the definition of *objections* and *stalls*. Objections are usually product-related reasons for not buying. (It's too expensive, big, little, green, old, new, etc.) Stalls are usually not product related ("I can't make a decision until after the summer" or "Call me back after Christmas" or "I'm not sure my employees would use it").

TURN OBJECTIONS INTO SALES
(continued)

When objections and stalls are blocking your sale, you must

- Uncover the *real* reason for not buying (a stall is not a real reason).

- Isolate each objection and stall, and handle them one at a time

If your customer tells you they like it, but they can't buy now, they really want to talk it over with their supervisors—what do you do? Realize that at this point, you don't know the *real* reason why they won't buy. Your goal is to isolate each objection (we'll discuss the method for this shortly). You can say to your customer, "Mr./Ms. Customer, I'd like to address each of these areas, because obviously they are very important to you."

> **Power Point:** You must handle each objection or stall one by one. Don't try to handle them all at once. You'll lose.

You will be overwhelmed, and your customer will become defensive. Remember to use the Diamonds on Velvet® method, and isolate each objection, as you did each product, one at a time.

Thanks to Bill Byrnes of RIA for developing and sharing the following:

The Objection-Handling Process

Do not skip any of these steps.

When you hear any objection or stall, do the following:

1. Keep Calm

Sit back. Make sure your body language reflects relaxation; don't lean forward or cross your arms. Keep quiet. Your customer may be expecting a rebuttal or a "but . . " from you, but it's not going to happen.

2. Let the Customer Talk

Allow the customer to say anything and everything he/she wants. Do not interrupt. Listen, and listen some more. Do not form any judgments or start thinking about a rebuttal. Wait until the customer has finished.

3. Acknowledge What the Customer Said

Make a very sincere statement, a simple concession. The customer may be expecting you to challenge what they've just said, but don't do it. Example of a concession: "Many customers initially felt this way. I can understand what you are saying" or "If I were in your shoes, I could see why this would be important." This helps relax the customer. They see that you're not going to come at them with a verbal bat. If their objection seems misguided, don't reveal that you think so.

4. Ask for Clarification

Ask some open-ended questions that start with what, why, where, when, who and how. Get the customer to talk. You want to identify and understand what the barrier is. Keep all your questions simple and your tone sincere. Do not attack—in voice or in body language. They need to feel comfortable with this process. Use this type of positioning statement: "Mr./Ms. Customer, I certainly want to understand what is important to you." Then ask a question about the specific objection—for example: "While you are thinking this over, what will you be thinking about?" or "What will be important to make this work?" or "Why do you feel that your employees wouldn't use it?" or "Why would it be best to come back in six months?" Based on their answer, ask at least one more question to ensure that you understand what's keeping you from a sale.

5. Confirm What You Just Heard

Repeat what your customer has just told you. Use the same kinds of words. Don't add or delete anything, just restate it. You want to show that you listened. This confirmation statement is your pathway to the sale, because you will find out if the prospect didn't see how they would benefit or make money. This will lead you to the final step.

6. Conclude and Close

Start asking closing questions. "If I could show you how you would increase your market share by using this product, would you be inclined to give it a try?" "Is there anything else that would prevent us from doing business?" If you get a Yes to the first question and a No to the second, begin re-merchandising your product, and once again align it with the information gathered during your needs analysis. Keep it simple and benefit-oriented. You should be closer to your sale.

TURN OBJECTIONS INTO SALES
(continued)

Tackle each objection or stall in this way. For each issue, go back to step 1. You must get past the stalls and get the real objections on the table. Don't give up! Don't let your customer sell harder that you do! If your product will truly benefit your customer, it's your job to show the customer how.

Sample Scenario

To illustrate how these steps can work for you, here is one example, and then you can try it for yourself.

SCENARIO: The customer has indicated an interest in an on-line information service for employees. They need access to up-to-the-minute information. Competitors are gaining a real edge by providing more accurate data to clients. You got positive confirmation during your presentation. As you start to close, you hear "It looks good, but I want to think it over. Can you leave some literature with me? I want to discuss it with my staff. Besides, we're really not ready for it yet. We're so busy. We might be able to start in a few months." Six objections! Let's get to work.

OBJECTION #1: I WANT TO THINK IT OVER

YOU: Mr. Customer, I can understand what you are saying. You want to be sure that this is the right service for you. In order for me to make sure you have everything you need, I want to be certain I know what's important to you. While you are thinking about using the service, what will you be thinking about?

CUSTOMER: A few things. Whether the employees will know the best ways to use it. I don't want to waste money if the service doesn't do what we need. And I have some people who have "computerphobia"; they are *glad* we don't have it. But they waste so much time looking up information.

YOU: I can see why this would be a problem for you. What kind of response time would you like to give your clients?

CUSTOMER: One hour. Right now it sometimes takes up to a day.

YOU: Let me see if I understand this correctly. You want to be sure that your employees will know how to use the service to ensure that clients' needs are quickly met. And you have some employees that have a fear of using computers at all, let alone using a computer service to do their job! Plus, you are not able to respond to your customers as quickly as you would like. Are these accurate descriptions of everything that is important to you?

CUSTOMER: Yes.

YOU: Mr. Customer, if I could explain how we can help train and support your employees, at the beginning and on a continuing basis, and enable them to provide information to your clients in less that 15 minutes, would that be of interest to you?

CUSTOMER: Well, yes.

YOU: Is there anything else that would prevent us from doing business now?

OBJECTION #2: NO MONEY LEFT IN THE BUDGET

CUSTOMER: Yes. There's no money left in the budget for subscription services. Our new year starts in six months. I like the fact that you can train the employees. And believe me, the response time sounds great! Call me back in a few months.

YOU: I can certainly appreciate that you don't want to go over your budget limit. Since this service is part of your customer-support program, could the cost be allocated from another part of the budget?

CUSTOMER: Hmm. Well, maybe in our training program. Or marketing costs. But I'd have to substantiate it to those departments and Finance.

YOU: Mr. Customer, if I could show you how all of the steps in our total training program are designed to coordinate with your own in-house training, and how the service can effectively serve the needs of your clients, wouldn't it make sense to get it going?

CUSTOMER: Yes. Let's see how you can do that.

YOU: Is there anything else preventing us from doing business?

CUSTOMER: No.

YOU: Merchandise, merchandise, and close.

Congratulations! You stayed on the path and made a sale.

TURN OBJECTIONS INTO SALES
(continued)

Now try a real situation from recent experience. Take any objection, and do a scenario to see how the steps work. Then, on your next call, try it live! You may want to write down the six key phrases as reminders for each step.

Objection: _____

_____

Let's say steps 1 and 2 are done. Now, what would you say?

3. _____

_____

_____

4. _____

_____

_____

5. _____

_____

_____

6. _____

_____

_____

Remember, do not skip any step! Practice, practice, practice. Keep handling the objections one by one. *Don't Give Up!* You will close more sales and overcome more Nos—in the workplace *and* at home.

> *"On the plains of desolation bleach the bones of countless millions who at the dawn of victory, sat down to rest and resting died. . . ."*
>
> —Joseph D. Ardleigh

CLOSE WITH A SERVICE-ORIENTED APPROACH

This issue separates consultative sellers from slick, "sell 'em and leave 'em" salespeople.

> **Power Point:** Consultative sellers always let the customer know, before walking out the door, what to expect from them.

Earlier, you learned the definition of consultative selling from the customer's point of view. Let's review this valuable concept again. Consultative sales-people:

▶ Sell their product or service and continue a relationship that began on trust.

▶ Provide on-going service to help support continuous success.

Before you walk out of the door, you want to ensure three things:

1. You understand the needs of your customer.

2. Your customer understands the value and benefits of your product.

3. Your customer knows how you will continue to service his or her account.

These things apply whether or not you make a sale. Your professionalism and thoroughness will follow you around. This is your reputation and the mark you leave.

CLOSE WITH A SERVICE-ORIENTED APPROACH (continued)

After the Sale

You want to verbally confirm the three facts listed above. You will want to develop your own words to do this, but keep it clear and totally focused on the customer. Here's an example:

> *"Ms. Customer, I appreciate the time that we've spent together. You have identified the areas of major importance to you, and I will keep your list of priorities in your account file. As we continue to work together, I will update this list as your needs change. I want to ensure that our on-going relationship always targets the areas that are most important to you.*
>
> *"My goal is to be of continuous service to you. Yes, I'm happy that we're going to do business together, but it does not stop here. I want you to always be my customer, so here's how I will follow up. I will call you in 30 days to make sure everything is working well for you. Then, I will call you every (name an interval that makes sense for the product or service you sell; maximum time lapse three months) to keep track of any changing needs or priorities. As needed, I will schedule appointments to review your current situation and recommend new product or service initiatives. How does this sound to you?"*

Always close with a service-oriented approach that fits your style. What works for you? Write it down here:

_____

_____

_____

_____

_____

_____

_____

_____

_____

NO SALE TODAY

Now, let's say that you don't make a sale. Of course, you want to keep your image as a professional. Don't walk out in a huff or show frustration (even though it may be justified!). You still want to hit home on the three facts listed previously, and add additional statements of intent.

Following is an example of closing with a service-oriented approach when the No Sale red light appears. Based on the particular reasons why you didn't get an order (wrong decision maker, not enough interest, special circumstances, no need for product, etc.), you want to keep the door open for future opportunities and referrals. You can adapt this sample script to your own style.

Power Point: Don't forget, the *final* image you leave with your customer will usually be the impression of you that remains with them.

"Mr./Ms. Customer, thank you for your time today. I appreciated the opportunity to learn more about your specific needs and to provide you with information about my organization. I would like to call you on (day and/or month), to keep informed about your changing needs. I will then be in the best position to recommend products or services that might be of benefit to you and your company. How does that sound to you?"

Power Point: If you have a call-back opportunity based on specific circumstances, set the appointment *before* you walk out the door.

NO SALE TODAY (continued)

What closing remarks would work for you?

Write them down here:

_____

_____

_____

_____

_____

_____

_____

_____

_____

_____

Remember, when customers truly believe that you have *their* best interests in mind, they will keep *you* in mind. When future needs arise, whom do you think they will call? Someone who quickly packed up and left? Or someone who demonstrated consultative selling? What would you do, if you were the customer?

PART

V

How to
Keep Customers—
for Life

KEEP CUSTOMERS

You made the sale. Congratulations! Now, we will look at how to keep your customer satisfied, and foster a value-added relationship to confirm that your customer made the right decision. Your goal is to have your customer for life.

You will consider what customers think about after they give you an order, what's important to their satisfaction, and meaningful ways to let them know how much you value the relationship. Finally, you examine what you can do to help them succeed. You will develop a simple plan for anticipating and supporting their ever-changing needs.

Customer Satisfaction: Beyond Customer Service

You've made the sale and you feel great! Now what? Your goal is to *keep* your customer. After the sale, your customer will decide if the benefits of your product or service fulfill their needs. This is a very important judgment. Should they continue doing business with you? Your product plus your personal service will help them make that decision.

You need to keep your customer satisfied. Before we examine the checklist of actions you can take to accomplish this, let's look at the difference between *customer service* and *customer satisfaction*. Customer service is delivered by you and your company. It is one or more actions taken to contribute to the customer's well-being. Customer satisfaction is determined by your customers. They will be satisfied if you have fulfilled their wants and needs and helped them succeed with your product and/or service.

You may think that your customer is satisfied because you've done a great job . . . in your own estimation. Don't forget, however, that it is what is seen (perceived) through the eyes of the customer that determines his/her level of satisfaction.

KEEP CUSTOMERS (continued)

Effective Service Checklist

Before you walk out of the customer's office, have you:

☐ Conveyed a service-oriented attitude?

☐ Assured your customer of how you will stay in contact?

☐ Advised when you will call next?

☐ Asked the customer if he or she has any special service requests?

☐ Let the customer know he or she has made an excellent decision?

☐ Confirmed that your goal is to keep him or her as a customer for life?

After you leave the customer's office, the ball is in your court. Your attitude and thorough follow-up will determine the level and quality of service to your customer. Here are some resolutions for keeping the mind-set you need to keep your customer satisfied:

☐ I will value the relationship with my customer.

☐ I will keep in touch with my customer on a scheduled basis.

☐ I will encourage customer feedback—positive and negative.

☐ I will respond quickly to any customer problems.

☐ I will handle any special needs.

☐ I will keep up-to-date records of customer service initiatives and results.

How can you make a positive impact on customer service? Since excellent service always shines, here are some important questions for you to think about. What sets your service apart from your competitors'?

1. When people buy from me, what follow-up do I provide?_____

_____

2. What can I do for or give to my customers that will be totally unexpected and appreciated? _____

_____

3. What can I say or give to customers that will enhance their opinion of me as a professional salesperson? _____

_____

WHAT HAPPENS IF A CUSTOMER HAS PROBLEMS WITH SERVICE?

In the real world, problems may arise that make it more difficult to keep a customer happy: defective products, shipping and billing errors, difficulty in using your product or service, and so forth. Be prepared for the good *and* the bad, and be prepared to help your customer. A lot of salespeople get very angry when things go wrong after the sale, and understandably so. You've worked hard to get the sale . . . and then something happens beyond your control. What you do next under these circumstances is up to you.

What are the barriers/difficulties in keeping customers satisfied? Write down your thoughts:

1. _____

2. _____

3. _____

What can be done? Write down your recommendations:

1. _____

2. _____

3. _____

For these situations, you may need the help of your manager or other individuals in your company. Discuss any problems and recommended solutions with them.

> **Power Point:** Customers expect you to fix problems. It's not their problem, it's yours. Don't blame others; provide solutions, instead. That's your responsibility.

If you are willing to do whatever it takes to give great service, chances are that your customers will continue to invest in your future.

KEEP COMMUNICATIONS FLOWING

Your on-going communication with your customers will have many benefits for both of you. Through communication, you will know when a customer is

- Happy with your product/service

- Unhappy with your product/service

- Receptive to hearing about new product/service information

- Using the product/service in new ways

- Needing help with your product/service

The only way for you to stay on top of all of this is to set up a service schedule. The service needs for each customer depend entirely on their purchasing cycle and specific needs, so you will be in the best position to determine the timing for follow-up. Some salespeople need to keep in touch daily; others communicate once a week or month. Whatever works best for you and the customer is what should be done. Just do it.

A very important point about communications: Always encourage your customers to contact you at any time, for anything. Even when you cannot answer their questions, you can get help from someone else in your company. Customers are more comfortable when they know you will help with any service requests or needs.

Some salespeople hesitate to call and follow up with customers, because they fear they will hear complaints. *That fear will surely help you lose your customer.* You want to hear about complaints before they worsen, so you can quickly do whatever you can to correct the situation. Don't be afraid that you might not know how to handle a difficult situation. You're not alone, so be honest about this with yourself and your manager. Excellent self-study resources are available to help you overcome this fear. Don't forget—you are an adviser *and* a problem solver, and in order to advise and solve problems, you need to communicate!

KEEP COMMUNICATIONS FLOWING (continued)

There are many ways to keep in touch with your customers. You can vary the methods, just keep it going!

- Telephone

- Mail (regular and overnight)

- Fax

- E-mail

- Telex

Some Welcome Communications That Are Important to Customers

▶ Send a confirmation-of-appointment card before your in-person sales call. Thank the customer for the courtesy of scheduling the appointment, and mention the date and time. This establishes your professional image before you arrive, and sets you apart from salespeople who just don't take the time.

▶ Send a thank-you letter, note or card after an in-person sales call. Let the customer know you appreciated their time. If you closed a sale, remind them that you welcome being of any service to them.

▶ If an administrative assistant helped you in any way, send a thank-you note. That extra gesture will serve you well the next time you call. And it's a nice thing to do.

▶ If a customer has a problem you're trying to resolve, call to keep them up-to-date on the status. It's very important to do this. Otherwise, they will not know whether you're doing anything about the difficulty and may feel that their complaint is not being addressed.

▶ If anything special happens to your customer—business anniversary, birthday, promotion, special event, etc.—a congratulatory message is always welcome. (Many office supply stores and catalogs carry books of perforated, faxable greeting cards). A note, card or telephone call will reflect your extra effort. Customers remember extra effort.

▶ Sending a note or letter with a published article that might interest or benefit them is unexpected and another signal that you are remembering their interests and needs. Always mention that you saw the article, thought of them and wanted to see if it would be helpful.

▶ Always let your customers know about new products or services that have potential use in their company. Your job is to keep them informed. Call and give them the updated information, and/or schedule an appointment to demonstrate the value of the product or service. Refer to their Customer Profile, Priority Sheet or other notes, as necessary, to determine if the new product or service will fit their objectives.

> **Power Point:** Compose your communications to fit your customer's style.

Some customers like everything to be formal; others want informality all of the time. Some prefer a mixture of both. Match what you know about your customer—sending a formal letter to someone with a relaxed, breezy style is a real turn-off. And be careful to maintain your image in both informal and formal communications.

Some salespeople say they just don't have time to do this, or they hate paperwork, or it's really not that important.

> **Power Point:** If you want to keep your customers, stay in touch with them on a regular schedule. If *you* don't take this time, your competitors *will*.

Don't forget—your customers are receiving sales offers every day. Keeping in touch helps you keep your customers.

ESTABLISH A PLAN TO HELP YOUR CUSTOMERS

In this section, you will learn how to be proactive in serving the needs of your customers. When you are able to anticipate customer needs and offer recommendations that get results, you have earned your stripes as a consultative seller.

Leo Cherne, former Executive Director of the Research Institute of America, made an astute statement many years ago. He said that any "business owner/manager who is not confused today is not thinking." Your customer faces a dizzying array of choices, and constant challenges to run a profitable operation. Everyone seems to be putting out fires, spending a lot of time reacting, and wishing for more time to think of creative ways to grow and increase profit margins.

What can you do? You must be *proactive.*

Power Point: Alert your customers to possible new benefits, new ways to use your product or ideas for changes that will help your customer. Your ability to forecast an opportunity or even a danger sign could mean the difference between profit and loss. Customers appreciate knowing that you are looking for ways to help . . . especially when they don't have to ask.

Here's a plan: It's easy as 1-2-3.

1. *Alert customers to published articles that may have an impact on their business.* This says you are taking the time to keep up-to-date. Make that telephone call to say, "I just read that . . . and I thought you might like to know about it."

   Suppose you know that your customer's organization is going to make a major purchase of a popular service. You come across an article that compares the top four providers of this service, and you call your customer. She has not seen it. You send the article and it gets discussed at the decision-making management meeting, and used in supporting their decision. You have aided their plan for utilization of the service.

2. *Help your customers network.* Become a business "matchmaker." Your customers all have unique ways to tackle a problem or capitalize on an opportunity. One customer's skills in one area may be a resource for another customer. Always call your customers before you give out their names; they will be flattered that you recognize their special abilities. Customers need networks of their peers, and you can be a valuable conduit.

3. *Ask your customer on a regular basis, "Is there anything I can do for you today?"* They may say no, but they will appreciate the fact that you asked.

What Can You Do for Your Customers Today?

Make a list of your customers and write down at least one way to be proactive.

Name of Customer   **Proactive Action Step**

1. _____   1. _____

2. _____   2. _____

3. _____   3. _____

4. _____   4. _____

5. _____   5. _____

"Just one great idea can completely revolutionize your life."
—Earl Nightingale

CONCLUSION

This book is designed to help you succeed. It is filled with many thought-provoking questions, recommendations and suggestions for using your talent and abilities.

My purpose in writing this book is to help improve your life. If you have chosen a career in sales, your challenges are many and your opportunities are everywhere. Once you develop a consultative mind-set, you *will* increase your sales. Give yourself a chance and just do it.

Although the concepts and principles discussed here can be used and adapted by anyone—after all, everyone sells—this book was written for you, the sales professional who wants to achieve greater success. Watch what happens when you become a consultative seller.

"The best is yet to be."

—Robert Browning

◆

I would welcome hearing your comments and success stories. Please feel free to contact me. Thank you, in advance, for your feedback.

Karen Mantyla
President
Quiet Power, Inc.
655 Fifteenth Street N.W., Suite 300
Washington, D.C. 20005
Tel: (202) 639-4040

OVER 150 BOOKS AND 35 VIDEOS AVAILABLE IN THE 50-MINUTE SERIES

50-Minute Series Books and Videos Subject Areas . . .

Management
Training
Human Resources
Customer Service and Sales Training
Communications
Small Business and Financial Planning
Creativity
Personal Development
Wellness
Adult Literacy and Learning
Career, Retirement and Life Planning

Other titles available from Crisp Publications in these categories

Crisp Computer Series
The Crisp Small Business & Entrepreneurship Series
Quick Read Series
Management
Personal Development
Retirement Planning

DATE DUE

NO.